GLASTONBURY
Maker of Myths

Frances Howard-Gordon

First published in 1982 by
GOTHIC IMAGE PUBLICATIONS
7 High Street, Glastonbury, Somerset, England, BA6 9DP
This edition 1997

ISBN 0 906362 42 3
A catalogue record for this book is available from the British Library

Cover photograph by Bill Godsafe:
the Tor from Wearyall Hill at sunrise.
Back cover: Gargoyle at the Abbot's Kitchen

Editorial service and setting,
in 11-point Acorn Monotype Garamond,
by Abbey Press Glastonbury

Printed and bound in Great Britain by Biddles Ltd, Guildford, Surrey

For Jamie, James, Josie and Cary

Picture credits

Samant Bostock   14, 19
Mary Caine   75–82
Chalice Well Trust   31
Jamie George   21, 30, 35, 52, 62, 67, 85
Bill Godsafe   9, 16
Barry Hoon   60–61
Frances Howard-Gordon   69, 89, 91, 93
Michael Mathias   34, 57
John Michell   51, 56
Sarah Platts-Mills   12, 13, 23, 64, 95
Bob Ring   25, 39, 41, 54, 63, 71, 74, 87
Somerset County Council Museum Service   53
Gunnvor Stallybrass, Quest Community   97
Brian Walker   103, 108, 109

"The Wheel of the Year" (page 99) is taken from *The Celtic Year: a perpetual solar and lunar calendar* designed by Joanne McMahon (Bandia Publishing, Ireland, 1997).

Contents

INTRODUCTION

This guide to Glastonbury is for those who want a simple, brief outline of what makes this small country town so special. It is also intended as a companion to walks around the hills and ancient buildings so that the myths and legends, history, beliefs and personal experiences associated with each particular site can be consulted along the way.

However, because Glastonbury is not necessarily what it seems and there are many layers and all kinds of mysteries and meanings here, I would encourage you to look and see with an open mind and experience this place for yourself. What you read in the following pages is merely a taste, a very brief and undetailed study to help you on your way. There are three books which I seriously recommend for more profound insights on Glastonbury. These are *New Light on the Ancient Mystery of Glastonbury* by John Michell, *Glastonbury Abbey: The Holy House at the Head of the Moors Adventurous* by James Carley, and *The Avalonians* by Patrick Benham.

Glastonbury is overflowing with fantastic tales of magic, mystery and imagination, quite apart from its rich and colourful history. Indeed, Glastonbury has something to suit every taste. There are ancient fertility rituals and a neolithic spiral maze; the Cauldron of Inspiration, the Holy Grail and the elixir of Life; a faery castle, a magic mountain and lights in the hills; King Arthur, the Round Table of the Zodiac, and the story of Creation; the oldest church in Britain, the coming of the Saints, and the Chalice of the Last Supper; secret passages, running water and inexplicable shafts of light; a megalithic moon-observatory, lines on the landscape, and a sacred egg-stone ...

Even though at first sight the myths and legends look like a jumble of fairy-tales, sagas, poems, inscriptions, belief validations and social morality, they turn out to have a common thread, a pattern which stays essentially the same. In the process of being passed on from person to person and from place to place, a myth is transformed, appears to be completely different, and yet retains the same structural principles. For example, the Cauldron of Cerridwen, the inspirational Muse of the Romantic poets, the Quest for the Holy Grail, and the Cup of the Last Supper—all these are transformations of each other, written at different times by different people, with a different narrative each time, and different symbols. Yet they are all preoccupied with the same theme. They are all speculations on the insoluble problems of the human condition, and they are all asking the same question: What is the meaning of Life? To whom serveth the Grail?

The Glastonbury Zodiac and the Twelve Labours of Hercules; Goddess worship and the initiation ceremonies of the Druids; the geomancy of Glastonbury Abbey and the accumulation of magnetic energy—all these myths and rituals are striving for the same thing: order out of chaos and unity out of contradiction.

At the end of the day it appears myths are what make up the genuine process of history. Myths are the backbone of a culture, for are not the reflections on such matters as life and death ultimately more important than chronicles of personalities and events which make up our history books? And do not these myths, these experiments in ideas, actually influence society and cause events to occur? But this leads us to the great paradox. Are people themselves the creators, or are we merely caught up in a never-ending historical process of myth-making, carriers of a culture passed on to us through the centuries?

In Glastonbury myths are being transformed and re-made all the time. Ancient customs and cults are re-discovered and revived here, threads are followed, webs are woven, boundaries of consciousness are pushed. Glastonbury is a natural sanctuary where the earth spirit is teacher. It comes alive in the weird and wonderful landscape, in the peculiar shades of light, in the changing seasons, in the air we breathe ...

The spiritual power of Glastonbury changes lives. But one core theme has emerged, in my experience, as a constant. When people come to live in Glastonbury, their intent is to live out the spiritual values of caring, sharing and living lightly on the land. Not everyone succeeds, for humility is required. But there is a community here, small but solid, whose participants include young and old, who continue to practise the values of goodwill and unconditional love.

Dawn mist

THE TOR

The myths associated with Glastonbury Tor are extraordinary. It has been called a magic mountain, a faeries' glass hill, a spiral castle, a Grail castle, the Land of the Dead, Hades, a Druid initiation centre, an Arthurian hill-fort, a magnetic power-point, a crossroads of leys, a centre for Goddess fertility rituals and celebrations, a converging-point for UFOs.

These myths are still very much alive today, although they are constantly being built upon and undergoing change. This is not surprising, given that this 500-foot-high conical hill is a most striking and inspiring landmark—visible at vast distances and yet invisible at certain angles close-by.

If you climb the Tor on a clear day, you will be astonished by the extent of the view: to the north you will see the Mendip Hills together with the city of Wells and its cathedral; to the west the island of Steep Holm in the Bristol Channel; Brent Knoll to the northwest; the Polden and Quantock Hills to the southwest, and the Black mountains of Wales in the far distance; the Hood Monument and Dorset to the south; to the east Alfred's Tower on the borders of Wiltshire, and Cley Hill—a hill famous for UFO sightings.

On a misty day you can experience for yourself what it must have been like when Glastonbury was an island—the Isle of Glass. From the summit of the Tor you will see only the swirling mists of Avalon with patches of green in between. What is now the flatness of the Somerset Moors and Levels has become watery marshes once again.

Prehistory

The mythology of the Tor reaches so far back into ancient times that it is impossible to give it a beginning. But if we try to look beyond Christianity and beyond the Celtic Druids, we may discover some of the truth concerning its origins and purpose. New information and interpretations have been coming to light about what was previously dismissed as *paganism*. As each new cult or religion supersedes another, so it tries to blot out what came before—such is the nature of conversion. This is what must have happened in the case of Goddess worship, a way of life which existed all over the world until at least the fifth millenium BC.

The Goddess took many forms and was represented in a variety of different aspects, but believers would see her essential nature in the harmony and balance of the natural order, the ebb and flow, growth and decay of life itself. She was evoked and celebrated on hills and mountains, these being her *seats* or *thrones* on earth. It is interesting to note that many early images of the Goddess have spirals on their breasts, resembling the spiral on the Tor. Spirals also symbolised the coiled serpent or dragon, both regarded as sacred in the old religion. The dragon or serpent represented the natural energies of the earth and the sky—energies which were cooperated with and revered. In the Shakti cults of southeast Asia and China, dragons and serpents were associated with clouds and rain, and the Sumerian goddess Tiamat was a sea-serpent and Great Waters goddess. The Greek *Mother of all things* was the serpent Eurynome, who laid the world-egg. The dragon was also regarded as a manifestation of the psyche in which the real and the imaginary are blurred and are, as in nature, only different aspects of life.

The maze pattern on Glastonbury Tor, similar to Cretan labyrinths, was created for ritual purposes long before the Druids are said to have used it in their rites and initiation ceremonies. Spiral mazes are deeply symbolic, their most usual interpretation being that of the soul's journey through life, death and rebirth. The seven-circuit Tor maze would probably have been made and threaded during the time of the Goddess religion. Although Philip Rahtz, who excavated the summit of the Tor from 1964 to 1966, has not committed himself to the existence of a human-made maze, he has said that if it is there, its probable date would have been around the second or third millennium BC. Archaeologists are interested but cautious, and presumably they will remain so until the maze is excavated. However, in the summer of 1979 Geoffrey Ashe made a long study of the Tor and concluded that the maze did indeed exist. His booklet *The Glastonbury Tor Maze* gives the evidence he found and shows the maze to be one of the great ritual works of early Britain.

Example of a Cretan maze

Therefore, if we visualise the Tor as a dragon, symbol of the Primal Mother and the place where the ceremonies of rebirth and initiation took place, we can imagine a ritual where the participants would come face to face with the Mother, enter into her subterranean darkness, chaos and death, and be reborn and nourished again by her life-giving properties.

Celts and Druids

Around the third century BC, the Celts founded two lake villages at Glastonbury and Meare (see page 35). Their burial ground was called *Ynis Witrin*, an old British name meaning *Isle of Glass*. Also in Celtic legend the name *Avalon* occurs, derived, it seems, from *Avalloc* or *Avallach* — a Celtic demigod who ruled the Underworld. However, Avalon also signifies apple-orchard or isle of apples, very apt for the cider-making county of Somerset. Apples were associated with the Goddess in many mythologies and with a western paradise where the sacred apple tree is guarded by the serpent or dragon. Some names for this paradise garden derive from an ancient root word meaning apple.

According to pagan British as well as Celtic lore, Avalon was the meeting-place of the Dead—the point where they passed on to another level of existence. Not only was Avalon a hill surrounded by

Faeries on the Tor

water, but it was also linked with *Caer Sidi*—the Faeries' Glass Mountain or Spiral Castle where the natural energies of the earth met with the supernatural power of death. In very ancient times Caer Sidi was described as the abode of Cerridwen, the enchantress who possessed the Cauldron of Wisdom, a goddess with powers of prophecy and magic (see Chalice Hill, page 23).

The remnants of stones scattered around the lower slopes of the Tor point to yet another possible use of this hill. It could have been used as a moon observatory in conjunction with the threading of the maze, for there is a good deal of evidence connecting megalithic stones with Druid initiation ceremonies.

To many the key document on the whole question of Glastonbury is the *Life of St Collen* by a Welsh saint of 650 AD. The manuscript tells the story of a Christian hermit living in a cell on the Tor who is visited by two emissaries of the Faery King Gwyn Ap Nudd. They persuade him to visit their king on the summit of the Tor. Because the hermit believes faeries to be demons, he takes holy water with him. He enters the other world of the king's castle, refuses to eat what is offered him, splashes holy water everywhere and immediately the castle and faeries disappear.

During the sixth and seventh centuries, a mass of Celtic sagas appeared concerning the heroes of Britain. These sagas linked the Faery King Gwyn with the Glass Island, and also with Annwn—the Celtic land of Faery, King Arthur, and the cauldron of plenty. However, the earliest reference to the Tor is in the Charter of St Patrick compiled around the middle of the thirteenth century. It mentions two lay brothers, a fact which suggests the beginning of a monastic settlement on the Tor, and if not that, then it at least points to a Christian interest in the place.

Megalithic stones on the Tor

More evidence that the Tor was a monastic site occurs in the thirteenth century in a charter of Henry III of AD 1234, giving permission for the holding of a fair "at the monastery of St Michael on the Tor." Faery fairs turn up in folklore time after time and they always appear to have been held near mazes, mounds, standing-stones, hill-forts or earthworks. There is still an annual Tor Fair in Glastonbury, but it is no longer held on the Tor.

Arthurian associations

The oldest story connecting King Arthur with Glastonbury is told by a monk of Llancarfan, called Caradoc, in his *Life of Gildas*. Queen Guinevere was kidnapped by Melwas, king of Summer Land (Somerset) who kept her at Glastonbury. Arthur arrived to rescue her with soldiers from Devon and Cornwall, but was hampered by the watery country. A treaty was arranged between the two so that Arthur

Apple-blossom in Avalon

and Melwas ended their quarrel in the church of St Mary—the Old Church—and Guinevere was handed back to Arthur. Glastonbury Tor would have been an obvious place for Milwas to have a fort, and excavations on the summit point to a hillfort of that period.

In a pre-Christian version of *The Quest of the Holy Grail*, namely the Welsh poem *Spoils of Annwn* which occurs in the *Book of Taliesin*, King Arthur and his company enter Annwn, the realm of Gwyn Ap Nudd, to bring back a miraculous cauldron of inspiration and plenty. The Tor is featured as the Corbenic Castle (Grail Castle) where the procession to the heavily-guarded grail or cauldron takes place. As the cauldron was associated in those times with fertility and plenty, it is very possible that an ancient fertility ritual was performed there, traces of which survive in the later legends of the Holy Grail. Another link between the Grail and the Tor is the saying that if a rainbow is seen over the Tor, someone has seen the Holy Grail.

In Arthurian legend Avalon was also the home of Morgan le Fay, a Celtic goddess or Faerie Queen, but she was more commonly regarded as Arthur's sister. Her name occurs in Celtic Europe as Fata Morgana in Italy and as Morgain la Fee in France. As Fata Morgana, she lived beneath the waters of a lake, leading one to suppose that the Lady of the Lake in Arthurian mythology and Morgan le Fay were at one time one and the same goddess. In volume one of her *Ancient Mirrors of Womanhood,* the author Merlin Stone draws yet another parallel:

> The powerful Fata Morgana was but another name for the holy goddess Fortuna ... and there are those who say that Fata and Fortuna were but other names for the Three who were known as The Fates, for are not Fata, Fay and Faerie simply other ways of saying Fate?

Archaeological chronology

Excavations on the Tor between 1964 and 1966 give us a chronological outline which, although open to varying interpretations, gives us something to go on with regard to dating the uses of the Tor through the centuries. Remains of graves on the summit dating back to the fifth and sixth centuries (the Dark Ages) suggest a pagan religious site.

Someone has seen the Holy Grail!

It could also have been a small Celtic Christian monastic site as the type of pottery found is common to other early Christian sites, although the large quantity of meat bones suggests that these were not Christian ascetics. A sixth century bronze head with a Celtic face points to metal-working on the Tor and the site could also have been used as a stronghold or hill-fort. The Celtic Christian culture probably derived from the late Roman way of life and certainly predates any settled Saxon administration.

The discovery of a wheel-headed cross confirms a Christian basis in the eleventh century (late Saxon, early medieval) and the preponderance of fish, bird bones and eggshell among the animal remains definitely supports the theory that a Christian settlement, with a hermitage, existed on the Tor at this time.

The first church on the Tor was probably of the late twelfth or early thirteenth century and was dedicated to St Michael—a dedication which was characteristic of such a hill-top site. St Michael, apart from being the ruler of archangels according to Christian tradition, was also the dragon-slayer and the personal adversary of Satan. Early Christianity believed the gods of the old religion to be fallen angels, or demons. The Christian church seems to have had a definite policy of building churches dedicated to St Michael on the old religious sites and sacred mounds. Since the Tor and its spiral maze represented the dragon, symbol of the Primal Mother or Earth Spirit in pagan times, the building of a church dedicated to the dragon-slayer was obviously meant to act as a powerful deterrent to any kind of pagan celebration.

In 1275 there was an earthquake and the church of St Michael crashed to the ground, hopelessly ruined. Another church was built and the tower or chapel, which is all that remains, dates to the fourteenth century, with some later alterations and embellishments. The markings on St Michael's tower show Michael holding the scales and St Bridget milking a cow. St Bridget was originally the Celtic goddess Brighde who, at her festival of Imbolc in February, presided over the lactation of domestic animals, sheep in particular. She was the goddess of fire, and probably also of the sun, of poetic inspiration, of childbirth and metal-working.

Tunnels and waterways

There are many stories, both real and imaginary, about a series of tunnels beneath the Tor. Jazz sessions used to take place in one such tunnel entrance in the early 1960s, but since then it appears that they have all been blocked up. However, the most famous tale is about a tunnel from the Abbey to the Tor. At one time some thirty monks are rumoured to have entered the Tor via this tunnel, but only three came out again, two insane and one struck dumb. Wherever these entrances begin and end, a point worth noting is that many experienced dowsers are convinced of the Tor's hollowness and the existence of a variety of underground springs forming a vast network of hidden subterranean waterways. It is also believed that the spiral maze is represented within as well as without, and that a Druid cave or temple lies within.

There is no mistaking the powerful elemental quality on the Tor. Some would describe it as a whirlwind, a vortex or meeting-point of energies in their purest and wildest form; others would describe a primordial dragon twisting, turning, and roaring to be let out. Please note this dragon can be calm and serene too.

Many visitors to the Tor have had strange psychic experiences there including suddenly leaping into the air, feelings of weightlessness and disorientation, or disappearing into subterranean passages. In 1969 a group of night-shift workers saw a saucer-shaped object hover over the Tor, and later, a big fiery-red ball appeared over the hill and then moved rapidly over Glastonbury. In 1970 a police officer saw eight egg-shaped objects in formation over the Tor. These cases were reported in the local paper. Sightings continue to occur.

Glastonbury Tor also plays a significant part in the alignment of sacred prehistoric sites known as the St Michael line. According to the renowned author and thinker John Michell in his book *New Light on the Ancient Mystery of Glastonbury*,

Geographically it is the longest line across land that can be

Avalon floods: the Brue near Cowbridge

drawn over southern England, extending from a point near Land's End in the far west to the eastern extremity of East Anglia. On or near its straight course lie major St Michael sanctuaries of western England: Glastonbury Tor, Burrowbridge Mump, Brentor, Roche Rock, St Michael's Mount, Carn Brea.

Paul Broadhurst and Hamish Miller, the authors of *The Sun and the Serpent*, have used dowsing to track for 300 miles the course of this enigmatic line on the landscape with fascinating results regarding Glastonbury Tor and its environs.

People who live in Glastonbury speak of the way they are sometimes impelled to go up the slopes of the Tor, while on other days they would find themselves unable to approach it. The Tor maze is often walked with the intention of solving seemingly impossible problems as its disorienting effect can lift the veil betwen dimensions. For some this leads to new perspectives on life. A day or so before childbirth some expectant mothers have felt a strong urge to climb the Tor and this has heralded the onset of labour. However one perceives Glastonbury Tor—as a magnetic centre, as a cosmic power point, as an ancient oracle or a fairytale castle—the evidence unavoidably indicates the existence of a prehistoric culture deeply concerned with the forces of the earth and sky, forces which were depended upon, utilised, celebrated and understood in a way which has yet to be fully re-discovered.

The soft round shape of Chalice Hill

CHALICE HILL

Between the Tor and the town of Glastonbury is a soft round gently-sloping hill with a particular quality of lightness and merry-making, peace and tranquillity. At the foot of its southern slope is the healing spring of Chalice Well. Like most places in Glastonbury, Chalice Hill has a great many stories to tell, all connected with the symbolism of the chalice. The cauldron of Celtic literature, the Arthurian quest for the Holy Grail, the Christian chalice of the Last Supper—these three powerful surviving legends all come together in Glastonbury to create a living image of ancient cultural and mystical beliefs.

Prehistory and Celtic associations

Celtic folklore is full of tales about a miraculous cauldron. It appears in *The Cauldron of Cerridwen, Bran, Diwrnach* and *The Spoils of Annwn*. It is always a cauldron of inspiration and plenty, a source of nourishment and renewal of life. It is a female symbol whether it be of the womb which nourishes and brings forth new life or the breast which feeds and nurtures. And the one aspect common to all cauldrons is that they were always presided over by a woman, three Muses or the Ninefold Muse—the Goddess in one of her many forms: maiden, mother or crone.

The name Cerridwen has been translated both as cauldron of wisdom and fortress of wisdom, *caer* meaning fortress, *cerru* meaning cauldron. Existing references to Cerridwen are scanty apart from the sixteenth-century text by the Welshman Elis Grufydd which recounts this myth about her:

Cerridwen gave birth on an island to a son called Morfran who was as black as a raven. But because he was so black, she worried about his future and wanted to give him a good start in life with a gift of the magical powers she possessed. So she began to prepare the Cauldron of the Deep, the cauldron known as Aven, from which three drops of liquid would provide her son with powers of foresight and magic. She prepared this cauldron by carefully observing the movements of the sun, moon and planets and adding the herbs, roots and the foam of the sea at auspicious times. But the young man named Gwion, whose task it was to stir the contents for a year and a day, watched over meanwhile by nine women, stole the three drops and swallowed them himself while Cerridwen was asleep. There follows an incredible tale of Cerridwen's pursuit of Gwion which ends with him changing into a seed which plants itself in Cerridwen's womb. Finally, after nine months of living with the hated intruder inside her, she throws the new-born baby into the raging waters.

In the poem *Spoils of Annwn* attributed to the Welsh bard Taliesin, King Arthur and his knights go questing after the cauldron of Annwn. They seek it by way of the Glass Castle. Nine maidens watch over this cauldron and the link here with Glastonbury is the appearance in the tale of Gwyn ap Nudd, King of the Faeries, who is

CAULDRN OF CERRIDWEN

already associated in legend with Glastonbury Tor. Another link
between the cauldron and Glastonbury is in the Welsh tale *Peredur*, a
story with a grail which is a cup and a source of food like the
cauldron. In this tale the name Avalon or Avallach occurs. Indeed, the
cup or cauldron is a universal symbol which turns up in mythology all
over the world. It features in Celtic, Egyptian and Chinese myths to
name but a few, and in the ancient Tarot divinatory cards. It is often
one of four magical talismans which are the sword, cup, stone and
wand. The grail, cup or cauldron is also said to represent the heart.

Medieval, Christian and Arthurian associations

In Christian mythology the Grail became associated with Christ and
the Last Supper. Medieval grail romancers told of a sacred vessel
being brought to Britain by Joseph of Arimathea. In these tales
Joseph of Arimathea is a centurion who obtains the grail as a
memento of Christ. He is imprisoned for forty years or more during
which time Christ appears to him and instructs him in a secret
sacrament performed with the grail. After his release, he journeys to
Britain with a band of twelve missionaries and entrusts the vessel to

what appears to be a secret priesthood. In these grail romances, the cauldron becomes the receptacle of the Eucharist—the food of eternal life—not in fact so far removed from its pagan symbolism.

In the Quest romances, set against a medieval background of knights and chivalry, Templars, troubadours and court ladies, King Arthur's knights go searching for the grail, here symbolizing knowledge of the soul and eternal truth. A host of magical visions and supernatural occurences affect Percival and Galahad, the two most successful knights in the Quest.

During the high Middle Ages, the worship of Mary, the mother of Christ, was very popular among English Catholics and the grail became her emblem. She came to be regarded as the source of inspiration itself. In more recent times the poet Alfred, Lord Tennyson, wrote of the chalice:

> *The cup, the cup itself from which our Lord*
> *Drank at the last sad supper with His own;*
> *This from the blessed land of Aramat,*
> *After the day of darkness, when the dead*
> *Went wandering over Moriah—the good Saint,*
> *Arimathæan Joseph, journeying brought to Glastonbury*

Some people see the chalice as a symbol of spiritual nourishment, a vision of purity and truth, a life-giving vessel of miraculous potency through which initiation into the mysteries of the universe takes place. There are others who take the legends and symbolism literally and believe wholeheartedly in a chalice holding the blood of Christ being brought to Glastonbury and buried by Joseph of Arimathea under Chalice Hill. Miracles of interpretation are possible in this area, particularly when parts of a belief system are at stake. And indeed it is also possible to see the chalice as a crystal ball reflecting to us colourful images of the past, pictures of ancient cultures and beliefs —all mirroring the same eternal need for an ultimate truth, a final key to the mysteries of life and death.

The Holy Thorn, windswept on Wearyall Hill

WEARYALL HILL

This long thin hill shaped like an animal's back and lying southwest, overlooks the town of Street and has extensive views over the Somerset marshes to the Bristol Channel. It has been compared to a great fish, a dolphin or whale rearing out of the sea-level moors around it. Indeed, there are traces of a wharf near Wearyall Hill showing that Glastonbury was once a port. The hill owes its name to the legend of Joseph of Arimathea and the Holy Thorn—a tradition still very much alive today as we shall see.

Prehistory

Wearyall Hill is famous as the home of the legendary Glastonbury Thorn, or Holy Thorn as it is often called. But long before Christianity endowed it with meaningful associations, the thorn tree had intensely symbolic connections. The hawthorn, whitethorn or May Tree, as it was known, takes its name from the month of May in which it usually flowers, and the word May derives from the Greek goddess Maia who cast spells with hawthorn under the name of Cardea. In ancient times, May was the month of festivities and merry-making, a time for trying out partners before making a choice, and the first of May was the date of the Celtic Beltane festival which probably originated in reverence for the Goddess as Beltis, Belit and B'Alat.

In the late first century BC, the thorn became associated with the goddess Flora and later with the English medieval practice of picking flowering hawthorn boughs on a May morning and dancing round the maypole. In ancient Greece the hawthorn was used to decorate the bride's nuptial bed and torches of its wood were lit at the altars of Hymen. In Turkey a flowering hawthorn branch was used as an erotic symbol, for its scent is looked upon as the scent of female sexuality. It was considered to be unlucky if the thorn tree was cut down and, indeed, in Cromwellian times it is reported that a Puritan was blinded by a flying wood-chip as he tried to cut the Glastonbury Thorn.

Celts and Druids

The hawthorn is the sixth tree in the Beth-Luis-Nion alphabet, an alphabet of trees and their magical properties which was orally transmitted down the centuries by the Druids, the Celtic priestly caste whose religion replaced that of the Goddess. In Welsh mythology the hawthorn is portrayed as a wicked Chief of the Giants, Yspaddaden Penkawr, the father of Olwen, 'She of the White Track'. Giant Hawthorn puts all possible obstacles in the path of Olwen's marriage, illustrating the taboo against marriage in the hawthorn month. Another association with Wearyall Hill is to be found in the *Mabinogion* where a Celtic Salmon of Wisdom is the one visible clue granted to the pilgrim on his quest. Wearyall Hill could be this Salmon.

Arthurian associations

In Arthurian legend Wearyall Hill is King Fisherman's Castle which can be reached only by crossing the perilous bridge over the river of Death, the river Brue which runs through Glastonbury. Pomparles Bridge is the *pont périleux* in French which lies between Wearyall Hill and the small town of Street. This is the place where Bedivere threw Arthur's magical sword Excalibur into the river after the Battle of Camlan, when Arthur returned to Avalon to be healed of his wounds.

King Fisherman was the guardian of the grail and he lay impotent and ill, pierced by a lance in the groin, waiting for a knight to ask the vital question: to whom serveth the Grail? In one version of the tale, King Fisherman dies happily in Sir Galahad's arms; in another Perceval cures him, and in yet another it is Sir Gawain. To pass through the gates of King Fisherman's Castle was to pass from this world into the next.

Christian associations

The Holy Thorn on Wearyall Hill is one of Glastonbury's most famous relics and the story of St Joseph of Arimathea bringing a staff made from hawthorn in the Holy Land to England, has been chronicled throughout the centuries. The story goes that after the Crucifixion, Joseph brought twelve companions to Glastonbury and founded the first church in Britain. When they reached Wearyall Hill by boat, they were 'weary all'. Joseph thrust his staff into the ground, it took root and a flowering thorn tree burst forth. The miraculous property of the thorn was seen in its flowering which was always on Christmas Day in memory of the birth of Christ.

The *Lyfe* of St Joseph, written in the early sixteenth century has this to say about the thorn:

> *Thre hawthornes also, that groweth in Werall*
> *Do burge and bere grene leaves at Christmas*
> *As fresshe as other in May, whan the nihtyngale*
> *Wrestes out her notes musycall as pure as glas;*
> *Of all wodes and forestes she is the chefe chauntres.*

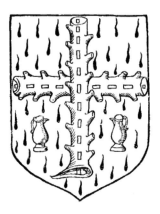

Late-15th-century shield adopted by Abbot Beere showing "a green cross raguly with blood drops and two cruets"

The tale of Joseph of Arimathea and the thorn is remarkable for its tenacity through the ages and its weaving together of pagan and Christian symbolism. Joseph's staff of hawthorn together with the Holy Blood which he is said to have caught from Christ's wounds on the cross in a cup or grail, is well illustrated. Abbot Richard Beere at Glastonbury adopted a new shield in the late fifteenth century which shows: 'a green cross raguly with blood drops and two cruets'. The green cross with shoots is obviously thorn. Joseph's staff and his carrying of the grail to England, both suggest fertility and abundance. The following popular rhyming couplet expresses this perfectly:

> *If Saint Joseph's Day is clear,*
> *We shall get a fertile year.*

The famous Thorn still grows at Glastonbury, flowering on at least three religious sites at Christmas time. Even though the original on Wearyall Hill was finally chopped down, a small windswept thorn survives in the authentic place on the upper slope. Significantly, the thorn is not native to this country, but is a Levantine variety from Palestine. A large thorn tree, a descendant of the original, grows in the churchyard of St John's on Glastonbury High Street, and yet another in the Abbey grounds. You can also see at St John's church Abbot Beere's shield in glass from the fifteenth century, and a fine stained-glass window depicting Joseph of Arimathea.

In continuation of the old tradition, a sprig of blossom is sent to the reigning monarch every year at Christmas and the ceremonial cutting of the thorn is done by the mayor in St John's churchyard. The Christian meaning can be summed up in this paragraph written by a clergyman in 1645:

> I knowe that England doe keep the right day that Christ was borne on, above all the Nations of Christendome, because we have a miracle hath often been seene in England upon that day, for we have a tree in England, called the Holy Thorne, by Glassenbury Abbey, nigh the Bathe, which on the 25 day of December, which is our Christmas Day, hath constantly blossomed, which the people of that place have received from antiquitie, that it was that kind of thorne, wherewith Christ was crowned.

In the Glastonbury Zodiac (see page 75) Wearyall Hill is in the sign of Pisces and its fish-shape is one of two, the other being at Street. Astrologically the Age of Pisces saw the beginning of Christianity and here, Joseph of Arimathea's staff being thrust into the fish, represented by Wearyall Hill, could be said to coincide with the birth of Pisces. Some see the staff episode as the entering of spirit into matter, a downrush of power which would have created a flashing force of immense strength.

The ridge-shape of Wearyall Hill complements the cone of the Tor and the dome of Chalice Hill. Wearyall is usually seen as the third hill or third aspect of Glastonbury. In this context the Tor is seen as dynamic power, Chalice Hill is love and Wearyall Hill is intellect in its original meaning of spiritual perception or creative illumination.

The thorn tree on Wearyall is highly regarded by the rich assortment of pilgrims to Glastonbury in the late twentieth century. Some say its magical properties can bestow healing and insight. In Celtic tradition, a rag or ribbon is tied on the branches of such a sacred tree to bring good luck or to make a dream come true.

The Holy Thorn in blossom on Christmas Eve

This stone is now on the riverbank nearby

BRIDE'S MOUND

Bride's Mound, though rich in history and tradition, is barely visible and difficult to reach. At the time of writing, it is covered in stinging nettles so tall they brush against your eyes, and it is located in the most unwholesome of places — right next to the sewage works at Beckery, to the right of the foot of Wearyall Hill on the way to Street.

There are many stories about St Bridget visiting Glastonbury in 488 AD. Both William of Malmesbury and John of Glastonbury write c. 1400 AD about her spending time at Bride's Mound, where there was an oratory dedicated to Mary Magdalene. John of Glastonbury also describes a chapel dedicated to St Bridget which had a special opening healing those who passed through it. Relics of hers were said by both writers to be displayed in the chapel. The fields around are still referred to as The Brides, and John of Glastonbury also wrote about "a monastery of holy virgins" on Wearyall Hill, telling a fascinating story about King Arthur having a vision at Beckery of Mary as Mistress of the Earth and Queen of Heaven, and her son Jesus. This is said to have converted him to Christianity.

It is also said in Arthurian legend that pilgrims who passed over Pomparles Bridge had to spend the night in vigil at the chapel on their way to the holy Isle of Avalon. As it is generally agreed by archaeologists that there was a wharf at the foot of Wearyall Hill, Bride's Mound could have been a kind of gateway to Avalon.

Philip Rahtz conducted an excavation of the mound in the 1960s and discovered some flints and pottery similar to that found in the nearby lake villages. Roman coins, bronze items and tiles suggest the mound was used throughout Roman times. Evidence of post-holes and wattle-and-daub structures dating from around 650 AD to 900 AD was found, as well as many burials, a Saxon stone chapel and priest's house dating to around 930 AD.

During the Celtic Revival of the 1920s, which coincided with a Glastonbury revival (see Glastonbury Culture, page 103), strange but undoubtedly real events occurred at what was called Bride's Well on Bride's Mound. This spring was marked by a stone and a thorn tree; objects were also thrown into the well for good luck. Two sisters, Janet and Christine Allen, friends of the Tudor Poles (Wellesley Tudor Pole was one of the founders of the Chalice Well Trust), had been guided by Tudor Pole's psychic insight to search in the water at Bride's Well at Glastonbury. Patrick Benham, in *The Avalonians*, describes the events as follows:

> It was while doing this that they retrieved a curious primitive-looking blue glass bowl ... Bride's Well itself was more like a rather muddy pond, into which the water from nearby fields used to drain through a sluice. However, it was certainly an ancient spot. An old thorn tree grew next to it on which generations of Glastonbury folk used to hang ribbons and other offerings to St Bride for the help of the sick or the barren ... There were several reports of cures and mystical

and revelatory experiences in the presence of the Cup. As time went on, forms of service were evolved which had points in common with church practices while giving a greater emphasis to the feminine mode represented by the Cup and the teaching of Spiritual Womanhood.

The events around this mysterious Cup came to a crescendo when the national press, tipped off by various London alumni, reported the discovery at Glastonbury of a mysterious Cup which, upon lengthy examination, they reported to be the Holy Grail.

All the legends and traditions associated with Bride's Mound and Bride's Well have one thread in common: the existence of a spiritual community of women in this area. Now Goddess revivalists are keen to resuscitate this site and a grassroots group of Glastonbury women called the Friends of Bride's Mound are gaining the support of English Heritage, Mendip District Council, Somerset County Council and the Antiquarian Society with a proposal to make the mound into a sanctuary with a garden of herbs and an orchard in keeping with its past. Beehives would also be appropriate, as the name Beckery originally meant "beekeepers' island". Of course this is a wonderful idea, and let us hope that it will come about. Then the visitor to Glastonbury will have yet another sacred site to enjoy and benefit from.

Morning mist covers the Levels like the marsh a millennium ago

Floods on the moors at sunset

THE LAKE VILLAGES

Here we need to imagine the Somerset Levels and Moors as they would have been in prehistory, dependent on the currents of a Bristol Channel much larger than it is now. In fact they would have been covered by sea until about 4500 BC, when the sea level gradually fell, turning the area into an esturine swamp colonised by reeds. Gradually cut off from the sea completely by the accumulation of silt deposits, a freshwater marsh developed. It is in this damp, but abundant, environment that the first evidence of human activity was found. A raised trackway was discovered in the early 1970s, preserved in the waterlogged peat. This, in itself, was not uncommon, but when the wood was dated using dendrochronology, it was found to have been felled in the winter 3807–06 BC. This trackway, raised above the water on wooden cross-pegs, runs some 2,000 yards, linking two areas of higher ground at Westhay and Shapwick. It was built in neolithic times using stone tools and completed in one season. It remains an important example of skill and organisation among our neolithic ancestors. (See *Sweet Track to Glastonbury* by Bryony and John Coles; *The Lake Villages of Somerset* by Stephen Minnit and John Coles; *The Peat Moors Visitor Centre* by Margaret Cox.)

The Glastonbury Lake Village was discovered in 1892 by Arthur Bulleid, a young medical student from Glastonbury who had become fascinated by the lake villages found in Switzerland. For four years he walked the moors and was finally rewarded when he found a field of raised mounds less than a mile northwest of Glastonbury on the road to Godney. Molehills revealed fragments of pottery, charcoal, bone and a whetstone, and in July of that year, when the ground was drier, he began excavating. The field was given to the Glastonbury Antiquarian Society, founded by Bulleid's father, and remains in its care. Many years of seasonal excavations were to reveal one of the richest Iron Age settlements in Britain. Two further settlements at nearby Meare were later excavated.

Some of the mounds of the Glastonbury Lake Village site marked the positions of round houses which had been repaired and rebuilt as the marshy conditions continued to intrude over a period of about 200 years, from 250 BC until 50 BC. Clay and wood had been piled up to create a dry area above the swamp, and each house had an elaborate foundation of layered wood, sometimes brushwood, and clay to further protect the occupants from the damp. The houses were made by driving a circle of posts into this firmer ground and weaving or tying wattle walls around them. The walls were then daubed and the house thatched with water reed. All the clay and wood would have been carried to the "island" by boat.

An abundance of potsherds were recovered from the Glastonbury site, about 95 percent plain ware and the rest showing finely made pots decorated with geometric and curvilinear patterns. An exceptional number of spinning whorls and weaving combs were found, indicating that they might have produced cloth for trade. We know from bone fragments that they kept sheep and so would have had their own wool. A wide range of wooden artifacts were found, including containers made in a variety of ways illustrating the skill and sophistication of their woodworkers. Lathe-turned parts of wheels have also been found. Evidence of bronze casting and ironworking were uncovered, including the very fine "Glastonbury Bowl" made from sheet bronze. Glass beads, shale armlets and other objects of bone and antler, including dice and a possible shaker, helped to further illustrate life in this watery settlement.

> The landscape of the Glastonbury Lake Village was a mixture of wetland and dry land. Arable fields for wheat, barley and oats were laid out on the dry slopes of the Glastonbury upland and the sand islands to the north. Some hoe plots for vegetables such as Celtic beans and peas were probably worked on the lower slopes. At the junction of the land and swamp, reed beds were harvested, and wildfowl captured here and on the more open waters. The raised bog to the west of the lake village attracted grouse and supported berries. The swamp and sluggish waters of the Brue yielded eel, fish and frogs; beaver and otter were also present in clearer parts of the water system. The shallow waters and damp ground at the edge of the swamp encouraged a variety of wild plants. Seasonal drying of low-lying meadowland and upslope pasture supported sheep and cattle. Upslope of this was woodland, coppiced in places. Above was the forest, used for supplies of timber and also for hunting of deer and forage for pigs.   *(The Lake Villages of Somerset)*

It is said that the Glastonbury and Meare lake villagers buried their dead on the sacred Isle of Avalon below the Tor, and this they did with great ceremony and reverence for the dead. This would account for the large number of Celtic legends about the Glass Isle as a Hades or Land of the Dead.

Discoveries of lake villages stretch from Asia Minor in the east to the British Isles in the west, and from Germany to Italy. In Britain and Ireland alone, several hundred examples have been recorded, and this fascinating almost forgotten way of living still continues in New Guinea, Borneo and Dahomey in Africa. Most of the Glastonbury Lake Village finds can be seen at the Tribunal museum (which also houses the Tourist Information Centre) in Glastonbury High Street.

Christian and Arthurian associations

Not far from the site of the lake village at Meare is the Fish House, which is thought to have been a house for one of the Abbey officials. As there were large lakes full of fish around this area, the official was probably in charge of the fishing. The house was built in the time of Adam de Sodbury in the early 1300s. He also built the Meare Manor House, which served as the summer palace for successive Glastonbury abbots, and the Church of St Mary, in which is a stone carving of the Holy Grail. The Meare lake is said to have measured five miles in circuit and a mile and a half across in 1539. Legend has it that this was the lake where Arthur's sword Excalibur first appeared, offered to him by the Lady of the Lake before he became king.

Peat Moors Visitors' Centre

It is well worth a visit to The Peat Moors Visitors' Centre, near Westhay, where the lake villagers' way of life can be glimpsed and even experienced through their finely reconstructed huts, spinning, dyeing and wattle-and-daub demonstrations. In 1996 a reconstruction was organized by Cary Meehan of a boat made from a single oak trunk. The original boat was discovered nearby at the former Shapwick railway station and dated to around 350 BC.

Glastonbury Lake Village as imagined in a drawing by M. Forestier

All that remains of the Abbey's central tower

THE ABBEY

In the centre of the town, next to the Town Hall, loom the magnificent ruins of Glastonbury Abbey, site of the first Christian church and oldest religious foundation in the British Isles. What is left today are the remains of an amazing past stretching back into prehistoric times.

The size of the church is particularly striking: the distance from the east end of the Edgar Chapel to the west end of St Mary's Chapel, previously connected with the main church by a Galilee or porch, is 580 feet. The nave is about 87 feet wide.

In 1907 the Abbey ruins were bought for the nation ("Country house for sale," was the tone of the advertisement, "with interesting ruin in garden") and placed in the care and keeping of a Diocesan trust. The trust was keen to excavate the site and in 1908 Frederick Bligh Bond, an ecclesiastical architect from Bristol, was appointed director of excavations. But Bligh Bond was no ordinary architect. He was also interested in psychic phenomena and during his appointment at the Abbey, the most exciting psychic detective work took place in the shape of his discovery of two of the Abbey's lost chapels, the Loretto and Edgar Chapels, and the revelation of the original Abbey builders' use of the ancient science of gematria—the translation of letters into numbers. Bligh Bond also experimented with automatic writing and received messages from long-dead monks who communicated, in a strange mixture of poor Latin and Early English, a whole variety of details concerning the layout of the Abbey and ecclesiastical life. In 1918 he published his findings in *The Gate of Remembrance* much to the horror of church and archaeological authorities, who dismissed him from his post in 1922.

Prehistory

If we accept that the earth has a nervous system made up of underground rivers, veins of ore and streams of terrestrial current, and that in prehistoric times a sophisticated science was in use which recognised the magnetism and currents of the earth, then we are open to an understanding of the ancient science of geomancy.

Pioneering investigations into the whole subject of Earth Mysteries have been carried out over the last thirty years. This area of research involves the study of ancient sites and their landscape including folklore, archaeology, ancient astronomy, geophysics, and geomancy. Fascinating insights have been gathered into the way prehistoric people must have lived and thought about their environment. Experienced dowsers have found that every prehistoric monument was situated at an important centre or intersection of streams of terrestrial current. Avebury and Glastonbury are on two such sites. Just as Avebury is associated with Silbury Hill, so Glastonbury Abbey is associated with the Tor. Silbury Hill and the Tor were once sacred sites which may have been used in ancient rituals for some sort of accumulation of energy. The monuments nearby such as Avebury and the Abbey site could have been used in turn to help generate this energy with the aid of the sun and planetary influences. This would have been accomplished by means of carefully

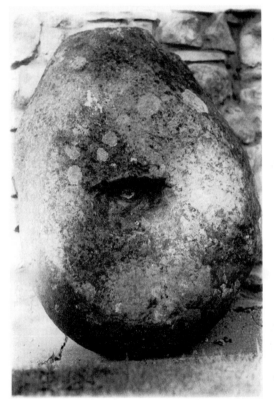

The egg-stone

positioned boulders, logan stones and alignments of standing stones.

One case relating to Glastonbury Abbey in prehistoric times concerns the omphalos or egg-stone. Omphalos means source of inspiration or centre of the world. The first recorded omphalos was at the Temple of Delphi (delphus is one of the Greek words for womb) —the spiritual and moral capital of ancient Greece at the height of its culture. The omphalos was the most universal representation of the Goddess, the pagan equivalent of the Holy of Holies, the vagina, womb or egg—source of life itself.

Bligh Bond's discovery of an egg-stone in the grounds of the Abbey gives credence to the idea of the Abbey as the site of a former pagan shrine. He described it thus: "It appeared to be roughly egg-shaped but flattened, the measurements being approximately 3 feet by 2 feet 4 inches by 1 foot 4 inches. One of the flat sides was exposed, and this was found to be artificially levelled over a considerable area. In the centre was a cavity, roughly hollowed." The stone found at the Abbey was supposed to have mysteriously disappeared, but there is a possibility that it has turned up again, leaning against the back outside wall of the Abbot's Kitchen, ignored like a piece of old unwanted rubble. It has been shifted about a great deal, and another cavity, on the reverse side, was probably cut to hold the shaft of a cross when Christianity took over. This Christianisation of pagan stones was common practice.

Christian associations and chronological history

According to tradition, in AD 63 Joseph of Arimathea together with twelve followers built a wattle church on land given to him by the local King Arviragus. He was given Twelve Hides (a Somerset hide is 160 acres of land) and his church was the very first Christian church in Britain, founded on the site of what are now the ruins of Glastonbury Abbey. This church became known as the *Vetusta Ecclesia* (old church) and in AD 160 two missionaries sent to Britain by Pope Eleutherius, named Faganus and Deruvianus, repaired the ancient

Antiquarian artists' impressions of the Old Church

structure. In 633 Paulinus, a missionary who converted many Anglo-Saxons, had the Vetusta Ecclesia boarded over and covered with lead in order to preserve the rapidly decaying fabric.

According to William of Malmesbury's *De Antiquitate Glastoniensis Ecclesiae*, in his account of Joseph of Arimathea building the Old Church, "the said twelve saints residing in this desert, were in a very short time warned by a vision of the Angel Gabriel to build a church in honour of the Holy Mother of God and Virgin Mary in a place shown to them from heaven, and they, quick to obey the divine precepts, completed a certain chapel according to what had been shown them, fashioning its walls below, circular-wise, of twisted twigs ... and it was the first in the kingdom. God's Son distinguished it with greater dignity by dedicating it in honour of his Mother." The Old Church was, therefore, dedicated to Mary. In the sixth century St David added a chapel to its east end. This was later enlarged as the Abbey Church of Saints Peter and Paul. Thus Glastonbury could have been the first home of the Marian cult in Britain and according to Geoffrey Ashe "there is no rival tradition whatsoever. When all the fantastic mists have dispersed, Our Lady St Mary of Glastonbury remains a time-hallowed title." This information about the Marian cult is strong evidence for a pre-existing Goddess cult at Glastonbury, for the Virgin Mary often replaced sites of previous pagan Goddess worship. (See page 94.)

Throughout Britain at this time there were small scattered groups of Celts who remained untouched by the Romans, and Glastonbury was one such place with its monastery and community of monks. A Welsh Triad talks of the Glastonbury Church as one of only three with the distinction of a perpetual choir. Music would have played an important part in monastic life, particularly the ancient traditional chant. John Michell writes on this at length in his book on Glastonbury, but here is a snippet:

> The twelve missionary saints who brought Christianity to Glastonbury were also twelve choristers. Part of the religious secret which they possessed concerned the magical power of music, and the nature of their music can be inferrred from a tradition in the Coptic Church, that Christianity prevailed because it inherited arcane musical knowledge and the twelve-part temple chant from the priests of Egypt.

Many Celtic saints and scholars were said to have visited the monastery including St Bridget, St Beon (St Benignus), St David and St Patrick. Even St Columba who brought Christianity to Iona and is credited with founding the Church of Scotland, is mentioned in connection with Glastonbury, and there is a story about St Patrick being the first abbot of Glastonbury.

Whatever the truth may be regarding who came and went from Glastonbury, the fact remains that when the Anglo-Saxons arrived here in AD 658, they found a little church 60 feet by 26 feet, an exceedingly old church patronised by Irish pilgrims. However, no-one could tell them who the original builders were. Under the Saxons, all the other great sanctuaries such as London, York, Lincoln, Amesbury and St Albans were looted and overrun. Only Glastonbury Abbey saw no break in its Christian continuity, passing intact from British to Saxon hands. Of course, by the time the Saxons reached Glastonbury, they were already converts to Christ, which would account for their benevolence to the Abbey. King Ine of Wessex continued to give grants and to enrich the Abbey in thanksgiving while he was defeating the Welsh under Geraint, occupying Taunton and annexing Devon and Cornwall.

In 704 the Charter of King Ine, in which he confirmed all previous grants and exempted the abbot's whole domain from episcopal authority, was signed in the wattle church. He also built a new church in honour of the apostles Peter and Paul, and enriched the old church but left it alone architecturally. Then Ine went to Rome and arranged for Glastonbury Abbey to come directly under papal control, for the Saxon religion by then was Roman, not Celtic. Nevertheless Glastonbury's Celtic roots persisted. The monastery continued to attract scholars from Wales, Ireland and Scotland as it did from among the Romans, Saxons and later the Normans. It remained an important Celtic shrine maintaining a mystique of its own until it was finally brought under Benedictine rule in the 10th century.

Under St Dunstan, who became abbot in 943, Glastonbury Abbey became the largest and wealthiest monastery in the land after Westminster. A popular saying at the time ran thus: "If the Abbot of Glastonbury could marry the Abbess of Shaftesbury, they would have more land than the King of England." Such was its reputation that its monks became abbots and bishops and it was described as a second

Rome. St Dunstan was the abbot (940–957) who established
Glastonbury as an important literary centre, for he was a great lover
of books and a scribe himself. He acquired many books for the library
at the Abbey. John Leland, the antiquary advisor to Henry VIII, was
an expert on monastic libraries and even he was amazed by
Glastonbury's enormous collection:

> I was a few years ago at Glastonbury in Somerset, where the
> most ancient and at the same time most famous monastery in
> our whole island is located. I had intended, by the favour of
> Richard Whiting, abbot of that place, to refresh my mind,
> wearied with a long course of study, when a burning desire to
> read and learn inflamed me afresh. This desire, too, came
> upon me more quickly than I thought it would. So I
> straightway went to the library, which is not open to all, in
> order to examine most diligently all the relics of most sacred
> antiquity, of which there is so great a number that it is not
> easily paralleled anywhere else in Britain. Scarcely had I
> crossed the threshold when the mere sight of the most
> ancient books took my mind with an awe or stupor of some
> kind, and for that reason I stopped in my tracks a little while.
> —Quoted by James Carley in *Glastonbury Abbey:*
> *The Holy House at the Head of the Moors Adventurous*

But regardless of its great wealth and fame, a mysterious quality
of 'otherness' remained at Glastonbury Abbey. Whether it was the
alchemical secret hidden in the floor of the Old Church about which
William of Malmesbury wrote: "Moreover, in the pavement may be
remarked on every side stones designedly interlaid in triangles and
squares, and sealed with lead, under which if I believe some sacred
mystery to be contained, I do no injustice to religion," or indeed the
most fascinating Prophecy of Melkin, from *The History of the Britons*
by the Welsh bard known as Maelgwn of Gwynedd. He was a
contemporary of King Arthur who died in 547 and was written about
in John of Glastonbury's *Chronicle*. The prophecy, originally in Welsh,
is translated here from the Latin by James Carley:

> The Isle of Avalon, greedy in the burial of pagans, above
> others in the world, decorated at the burial place of all of

them with vaticinatory little spheres of prophecy, and in future it will be adorned with those who praise the Most High. Abbadare, powerful in Saphat, most noble of pagans, took his sleep there with 104,000. Among them, Joseph de Marmore, named 'of Arimathea' took everlasting sleep. And he lies on a forked line close to the southern corner of the chapel with prepared wattle above the powerful venerable Maiden, the thirteen aforesaid sphered things occupying the place. For Joseph has with him in the tomb two white and silver vessels filled with the blood and sweat of the prophet Jesus. When his tomb is found, it will be seen whole and undefiled in the future, and will be open to all the earth. From then on, neither water nor heavenly dew will be able to be lacking for those who inhabit the most holy island. For a long time before the Day of Judgement in Josaphat will these things be open and declared to the living.

Both John Michell and James Carley remark on the alchemical symbolism in this text. John Michell in his *New Light on the Ancient Mystery of Glastonbury* interprets the symbolism thus:

> The reference to heavenly dew is to that *ros coeli* of the Rosicrucians which distills the pure gold and is symbolized by the droplets in St Joseph's coat of arms. In keeping with the eastern character of the Prophecy is the promise of "water and heavenly dew" to the inhabitants of the Isle of Avalon. Superficially, this offers little benefit to those who live in watery Somerset, but the phrase did not originate there. It makes more sense in arid Jerusalem, and one of the legends of the Jerusalem Temple is that, when the Jews rebuild it, water and heavenly dew are among the blessings which shall follow. Symbolized by the phrase are the happiness and prosperity which traditionally follow upon the restoration of the Grail.

In 1184 fire destroyed the whole of the Abbey church, the old wattle church and the greater part of the monastery. The ruins we see today are, therefore, fragments of buildings dating from the late twelfth century right through to the sixteenth which replaced the ones destroyed by the fire. Henry II was determined to rebuild the whole place at his own expense, but it took 120 years before rebuilding and dedications were finished. The first building to be constructed was the Church of St Mary in 1184, known as the Lady Chapel and built on the exact site of the Old Church. Large parts of this beautiful Chapel can be seen today. Even though the proportions of the Abbey were already huge and complex, each Abbot felt compelled to erect some new structure. In the fourteenth century, the cloisters and dormitory were rebuilt and the Abbot's Kitchen constructed. In 1497 Abbot Richard Beere built the Edgar Chapel and personally entertained King Henry VII at the monastery. In fact, many monarchs visited the Abbey over the centuries until Henry VIII put an end to all reverence for monasteries. Casting off the Pope's authority and declaring himself head of the Church of England, Henry began the violent period of the Dissolution of the Monasteries.

Chapel of St Mary, about 1910

At Glastonbury the episode was particularly horrific as the sixtieth abbot, Richard Whiting, refused to surrender the Abbey treasures to Henry's henchman, Cromwell. Savagery ensued. Abbot Whiting was dragged up the Tor to the summit where a gallows had been erected. Not only was his head chopped off and stuck on the Abbey gate, but his body was hacked into four pieces, exhibited respectively at Wells, Bath, Ilchester and Bridgwater. This marked the end of the Abbey, for no further attempts were made to preserve it. Cash was the priority, and workmen proceeded to melt, tear down and auction off everything of any value. A great deal of Abbey stone was used as foundations for the road between Glastonbury and Wells. A century later, a Flemish community attempted to take up residence at the Abbey, but survived only a few years. Desolation ensued.

Arthurian associations

It is only in the Middle Ages that King Arthur's association with Avalon is actually examined. Before that Arthurian legends were transmitted orally and through poems and the occasional tale mainly about his prowess in battle, and he was seen variously as a wind-spirit, a leader of the Wild Hunt with Gwyn ap Nudd riding through the thunderclouds in search of the souls of the Dead, or as a god of fertility.

Geoffrey of Monmouth in his British History (1135–1140) wrote simply: "Arthur's last earthly destination was Avalon." The Old French romance *Perlesvaus*, translated by Sebastian Evans as *The High History of the Holy Grail* has this note:

> The Latin from whence this History was drawn into Romance, was taken in the Isle of Avalon, in a holy house of religion that standeth at the head of the Moors Adventurous, there where King Arthur and Queen Guinever lie.

Giraldus Cambrensis, the historian with a critical attitude to Arthurian folklore, visited the Abbey himself to check on the facts of Arthur's burial and tells us the following story: Henry II learned from a Welsh bard that King Arthur was buried in Glastonbury Abbey and duly passed the information on to the then abbot. Later, after the fire

Arthur's cross (from Camden's painting)

and around 1190, excavations were undertaken and the remains of Arthur and Guinevere were unearthed.

Sceptics have tried hard to discredit the story of Arthur being buried at Glastonbury Abbey by pointing to the monks' need for publicity to attract funds for rebuilding. Yet the story stands up to scrutiny and Dr. Ralegh Radford who excavated the site between 1962 and 1963, has checked that an important person of the right period was indeed buried there and that there is no real reason why the monks should have invented such a fraud, all their details being accurate as far as he could tell.

The monks' story was as follows: around 1191 a particular monk wished to be buried in a certain place in the Abbey grounds and so the site was excavated in preparation. The diggers discovered a stone slab and a lead cross sixteen feet below ground level. On the cross was an inscription which read "Here lies buried the renowned King Arthur with Guinevere in the Isle of Avalon." Underneath it were two large hollowed-out oak coffins with the bones of a tall man inside. His skull showed signs of death by a blow to the head. The smaller bones and remains of yellow hair were explained as belonging to Guinevere.

Not long after this eventful discovery, Gerald of Wales wrote:

> Now the body of King Arthur, which legend has feigned to have been transferred at his passing, as it were in ghostly form, by spirits to a distant place, and to have been exempt from death, was found in our own days at Glastonbury, deep down

in the earth and encoffined in a hollow oak between two
stone pyramids erected long ago in the consecrated graveyard,
the site being revealed by strange and almost miraculous signs;
and it was afterwards transported with honour to the Church
and decently consigned to a marble tomb ...

Although it has since disappeared, the cross undoubtedly existed, for
in about 1607 Camden drew a picture of it and it has been traced to
an eighteenth-century resident of Wells. The remains of this early
grave were treated as sacred relics and reverently placed within the
church. Later, during rebuilding after the fire, a stately black marble
mausoleum was erected at the east end and the relics placed within.
Froissart, the French court chronicler, tells us of the romantic
pilgrimage taken by King Edward I and his young Queen Eleonor to
Arthur's tomb at Glastonbury in 1278. At the centre of the Abbey
church an inscription marks this spot.

Among the countless tributes to Glastonbury written over the
centuries, perhaps William Blake's painting *Joseph of Arimathea among the
Rocks of Albion* and his poem *Jerusalem*, which was inspired by
Glastonbury, stand out in more recent times:

>   *And did those feet in ancient time*
>   *Walk upon England's mountains green?*
>   *And was the holy Lamb of God*
>   *On England's pleasant pastures seen?*

For those interested in the ancient science of gematria, there is a
wealth of symbolism and meaning to be discovered in the
measurements and configurations of the Abbey and its environs. An
ancient connection with Stonehenge is indicated by the main axis of
Glastonbury, the straight line through the nave and tower of St
Benedict's church, along the length of the Abbey, up Dod Lane and
past the foot of the Tor to St Michael's church on Gare Hill in
Wiltshire. Extended further eastward, the 'ley' runs very close to

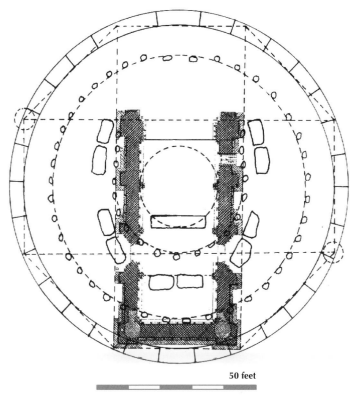

50 feet

The plan of the Glastonbury chapel with its octagonal geometry and the ground plan of Stonehenge, both to the same scale

Stonehenge. The original church, supposedly founded by St Joseph, was probably designed to point precisely to Stonehenge.

Even more fascinating is the geometric link between the foundation patterns of Glastonbury and Stonehenge. John Michell researched this at length in his *New Light on the Ancient Mystery of Glastonbury*:

> It can now be shown (with the closest approach to certainty that is possible in these matters) that Stonehenge and Glastonbury were both founded on the same pattern. This does not imply that the Glastonbury founders copied the plan of the ancient temple, but rather, that the same traditional model was used in both cases. It is impossible to say whether that model was transmitted by a freemasonry of temple builders over the two thousand years which separate

Stonehenge from Glastonbury, or whether it was renewed by revelation at the beginning of the Christian era. However one explains it, the evident fact is that both Stonehenge and Glastonbury share a common groundplan.

There are those who see monks from the past and hear their voices as they walk around the Abbey ruins. There are others who believe the ancient prophecy and envisage a glorious future when Joseph's tomb is found. But as it is with its majestic old trees, vast lawns and noble history, Glastonbury Abbey retains a magic quality and unique atmosphere which never falters.

Glastonbury Abbey has a fine museum; you can say a prayer in St Patrick's Chapel; in the summer months a monk demonstrates medieval baking in the Abbot's Kitchen; and miracle plays take place on July evenings.

The Abbey House, the building at the east end of the ruins dating from 1825, is now the Bath and Wells diocesan retreat house. Contact the warden about booking a retreat.

The Abbot's Kitchen, through the arches

THE ABBEY BARN

Though Glastonbury Abbey's estates were vast, the Abbey Barn is surprisingly small. It was used for storing produce from the complex farming system of the 800-acre Glastonbury Manor estate. Tree-ring dating of the Abbey Barn timbers has suggested the 1340s, when the Abbey would have been rebuilt after its destruction by fire, and would also have been internationally famous for its wealth and antiquity.

Although the Barn is not as large as other monastic barns, the sculptured detail of the masonry is exceptional, with emblems of Evangelists carved on each gable and human heads surmounting the buttresses said to be benefactors of the Abbey: one sculpture depicts Edward III (1327–1377). Animals and finials stand guard over the porches, and the intricate mouldings on the gable windows are fine examples of early 14th-century work. But by far the most outstanding feature of the Barn is its roof, which was built by traditional medieval methods. The Barn is 93 feet long and 33 feet wide; the roof was created to fit over this large area by using eight double tiers of crucks rising from the walls, with intermediate timbers to support the heavy stone tiles of the roof.

In 1975 a group of local residents formed a society called the Friends of the Abbey Barn. Their aim was to bring to life the Barn and its surrounding buildings by recreating the old farming environment. The Somerset Rural Life Museum was opened and, with funds from Somerset County Council, the buildings were rebuilt and restored, with appealing results.

The magnificent roof of the Abbey Barn

Now there are geese, chickens and sheep on the grass outside the Barn. Inside it are fine examples of old farm machinery. There are cider presses, withies grown in Somerset and used for basket-making, peat dug since ancient times—all with descriptions of the methods and processing used. In the courtyard at the back of the Barn are colourful examples of 18th- and 19th-century Somerset farm wagons, slurry pumps, a barrel washing-machine made around 1910, and some interesting machines for carpentry and joining.

In the Rural Life Museum the visitor is taken through all the stages of Victorian farming methods from the machines used to prepare the land, planting and sowing, harvesting, processing the crop, through to the actual marketing. Traditional local activities such as willow growing, mud horse fishing, peat digging and cider making are illustrated. Another building is the Abbey Farmhouse—also a permanent exhibition centre with a fine Victorian kitchen and a dairy where cream, butter and cheese were made. An exhibition depicting the life of a Victorian farm labourer from the nearby village of Butleigh with fascinating tape recordings of reminiscences of life in Somerset at the beginning of the century are in the museum's collections.

Volunteers help to welcome visitors to the museum and lectures, plays, exhibitions and demonstrations throughout the year help to make the Barn and Rural Life Museum a stimulating experience.

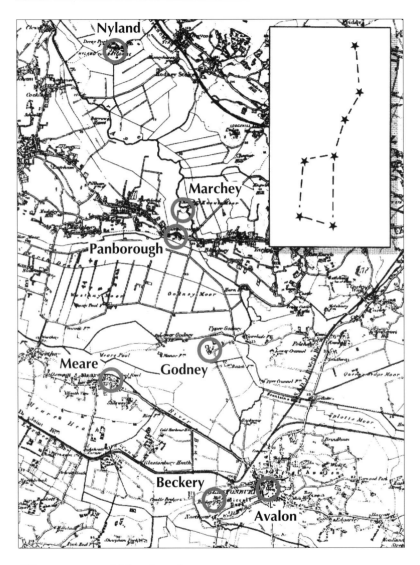

*The seven sacred islands and
the Great Bear constellation*

The Tor rising from a watery landscape

THE SEVEN SACRED ISLANDS

You will have noticed by now on your journey around Glastonbury that a watery landscape figures prominently in almost all the legends and history of this area. Since the earliest times there were island settlements in the Glastonbury waterlands. As early as 3800 BC wooden trackways were laid down across the marshes to connect these islands to each other.

We know that English kings continued to assert the total supremacy of the Abbot of Glastonbury over his domain and this was confirmed by the Domesday Survey. Seven islands within the

Twelve Hides of Glastonbury held special status and were exempt from taxation. King Edgar's charter of the tenth century listed the following islands alongside Glastonbury Isle of Avalon: *Bekaria quae parva Hibernia dicitur, Godeneia, Marteneseia, Ferramere, Padenaberga, et Andredeseia.* In English these are: Beckery (also known as Little Ireland), Godney or God's Island, Martinsea or Marchey, Ferramere or Meare, Panborough and Andrewsea or Nyland. In Celtic times these seven islands were inhabited by hermits; in medieval times each of them had a chapel on top. The monks of Glastonbury Abbey preserved and maintained these chapels.

Why were these seven islands so special? And how were they linked? John Michell, in his *New Light on the Ancient Mystery of Glastonbury*, appears to have solved the mystery. He sees them as seven sacred island sanctuaries and explains his findings thus:

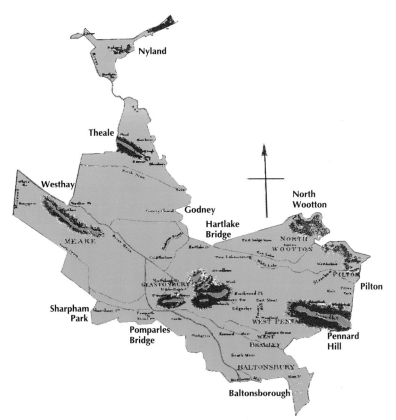

The Twelve Hides of Glastonbury, according to Warner in 1826

The answer emerges when the seven islands are plotted together on a map. They form a pattern which closely approximates to the pattern of the seven stars in the Great Bear constellation. Glastonbury corresponds to the star Dubhe on which the constellation pivots... The constant veneration by the Glastonbury monks suggests that they knew the secret of their symbolic arrangement... It is clear from their traditions, however, that the sanctity of the seven islands was recognized before Christian times. The first people who saw their likeness to the Great Bear would have been those whose eyes were trained to observe nature's symbolism, and that implies that the early tribes of Glastonbury, who journeyed in their imaginations across a stellar landscape, were the first to detect in their watery realm those particular seven islands which reproduce the Great Bear.

The relevance of this constellation of island sanctuaries to the history and mythology of Glastonbury is immediately apparent. From very early times the Great Bear has been associated with King Arthur. Welsh scholars derive Arthur's name from 'Arth Fawr', the Great Bear, and he is also associated with Arcturus, the brightest star in the northern hemisphere, whose position in the sky is indicated by the last two stars in the tail of the Great Bear.

I refer you to John Michell's book for more detailed information on this stellar myth and would only end by saying that early Welsh chroniclers associated King Arthur's Round Table with the Great Bear and suggested this celestial design was in some form imprinted on Earth.

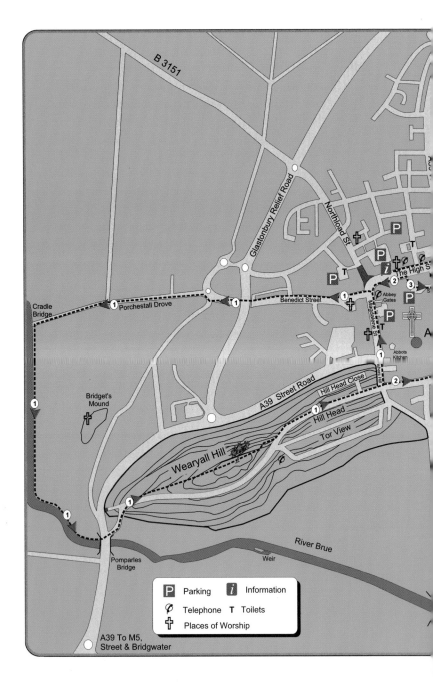

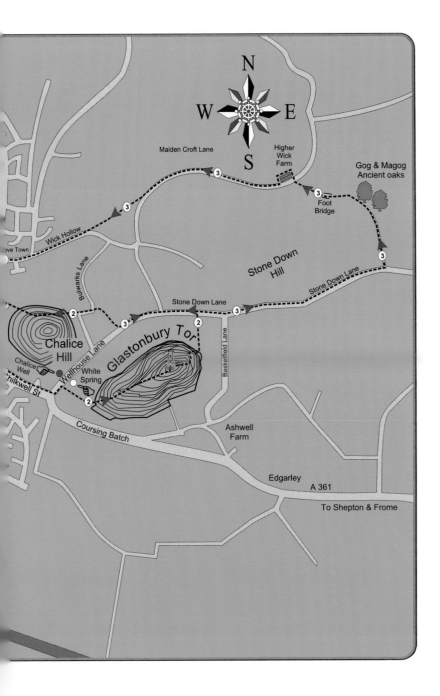

The well cover at Chalice Well

Red running water at Chalice Well

CHALICE WELL

At the foot of Chalice Hill, nestling in a valley between Chalice Hill and the Tor, lie the Chalice Well Gardens. The Well itself is to be found at the top of the garden, a garden beautifully cared for by the Chalice Well Trust. In 1912 what was a Catholic seminary at Chalice Well was bought by a remarkable visionary and Celtic revivalist called Alice Buckton. She proceeded to run a programme of plays based on ancient lore and legend, in her words "planned on the lines of the old religious Folk and Mystery Plays, with the aim of celebrating and making beautiful in various ways the Greater Festivals of the year,

Dragon statue at Chalice Well

from Carol Singing to the Festival of the Mid-summer Bon-fire."
After her death, the property was bought and the Chalice Well Trust
set up in 1958 by the mystic Wellesley Tudor Pole and his friends.
Tudor Pole sponsored Philip Rahtz's excavations on the summit of the
Tor and was the originator of the Silent Minute during World War II.

The source of the water is unknown but is thought to be in the
Mendip Hills some miles to the north. The water fills the five-sided
well-chamber and flows from the spring through a separate pipe
underneath the garden, and out through the lion's head. It has a high
chalybeate (iron) content and flows at an unceasing 25,000 gallons per
day at a constant temperature of 52 degrees Fahrenheit. Its supply has
never been known to fail even in the severest drought.

The waterfall cascades down, enters Arthur's courtyard and flows into the Pilgrim's Bath where many forms of healing have taken place. Flowing underground again, it finds its way to the pool at the foot of the garden where it proceeds to join other underground streams flowing under the Abbey grounds to where the Chaingate Mill in Magdalene Street once stood.

Prehistory

The convincing evidence for a spiral maze on the slopes of the Tor and the hill's ritual use in neolithic times strongly suggests that the ever-flowing water, which appeared as a spring at Chalice Well, indicates a site of some potency. Springs and wells, especially if they were situated close to sacred hills or mountains, were looked-to throughout pre-Christian times for their magical and life-giving properties.

Ancient holy wells were usually tended by an old wise woman skilled in healing and counsel and, like an anchoress, she would live at the well. Chalice Well would therefore most likely have been a healing spring from earliest times. For those interested in Goddess symbolism, the reddish colour of the water suggests the flow of blood at menstruation or childbirth, the blood of creation. The water can also symbolise the womb-waters of the Goddess or the water of Life.

Sir Norman Lockyer, the astro-archaeologist, pointed out that Chalice Well is orientated towards the East—the summer solstice sunrise—a precise time of pagan religious celebration and ritual sacrifice all over the world.

Celts and Druids

It is likely that the Celtic priesthood known as Druids may have founded a college of instruction at Glastonbury. They could have settled near this spot where an avenue of yew trees suggests its use as a processional path in ancient times. There is also evidence for an early anchorite sanctuary here. Perhaps in reference to them, a former nearby inn was called the Anchorage.

Arthurian associations

Gradually the Graal, Grail and Chalice came to mean one and the same thing: a secret to be discovered, an honour to be gained by proving oneself worthy. In the late 1120s William of Malmesbury, a monk of Malmesbury Abbey, was asked to write a history of Glastonbury Abbey and he was given complete freedom to use the archives. He records seeing several ancient manuscripts there about King Arthur. One of his marginal notes could well relate to Chalice Well. It is attributed to Gildas (AD 516–570) from *The Illustrious Acts of King Arthur*: "In the Quest of a certain Knight called Lancelot of the Lake ... a hermit revealed to Waleran the mystery of a certain fountain that changed its taste and colour frequently, which miracle should not cease until there should come a great lion ..." Mention of the spring is to be found in *The High History* of the thirteenth century and in Thomas Malory's *Morte D'Arthur* of the fifteenth century. Lancelot and other survivors are said to have retired to hermitages in a small valley near Glastonbury. This could be the valley between the Tor and Chalice Hill—the site of what is now Chalice Well.

Archaeological chronology and Christian associations

Chalice Well used to be 'Chalk' Well (hence the name of Chilkwell Street leading to it). In early place-names this often means limestone and can signify a cold spring. It has also been called the Blood Spring because of its reddish water, though by Christian times it had come to be regarded as the blood of Christ, not the blood of menstruation or birth. Along with the legend of Joseph of Arimathea bringing the Chalice of the Last Supper to Glastonbury in AD 37 goes the idea that he buried it in the earth by the well or under the well itself—a variation on its being buried under Chalice Hill. Symbolically, as the water runs through the chalice containing the blood of Christ, so the water mixed with the blood has supernatural healing properties.

The first mention of healing waters at Glastonbury occurred in 1582 when the famous astrologer and mathematician Doctor John Dee announced his find of the "*Elixir Vitae*" at Glastonbury. In 1750

The Lion's Head

a certain Matthew Chancellor made a sworn statement about how he had suffered from asthma for thirty years, but had been cured by drinking a quarter-pint of Chalice Well water each Sunday morning for seven consecutive Sundays. The story spread like wildfire and in the month of May, ten thousand visitors descended on the Well to drink and bathe. A special healing bath was erected and Chalice Well became a popular spa. The bath can still be seen in the Gardens today.

Many intriguing stories are connected with Chalice Well, and I refer you to *The Avalonians* by Patrick Benham. But there is one story I must mention briefly in its context here. In 1907 a certain prophecy concerning the Holy Grail came to light. Three maidens were to find the Cup and its revelations would have profound impact on women's spirituality. Indeed they did find a blue glass bowl under strange circumstances; it even baffled British Museum experts and led to the national press calling it the Holy Grail (see page 32). This Cup resides at the Chalice Well, discreetly secured by the Trust.

After the First World War, a wrought-iron well cover designed by Frederick Bligh Bond, the architect and clairvoyant who carried out the first excavations in the Abbey, was presented as an offering for peace. Carved on this elaborate cover is a major religious symbol called the *Vesica Piscis*, two interlocking circles—a design used in many significant ancient buildings including prehistoric monuments.

The Vesica Piscis was first adopted by the early Christian church and represents the interpenetration of the material and immaterial worlds or the yin and the yang where the conscious and unconscious meet. The intersection between the two circles gives the *piscis* (fish) or mandorla, also called the yoni, a shape representing the female genitals which in ancient times were regarded as the gate of earthly existence and spiritual knowledge. It is also seen as the blending of masculine and feminine.

Another Vesica Piscis, formed in wrought ironwork over the large wooden door leading to Arthur's Courtyard, shows the modern Christian mystical interpretation of the symbol. This Vesica Piscis has a sword running through the centre, symbol of will or rationality, the sword of the dragon-slayer. A line of water runs underneath depicting the Aquarian age.

For many years the Chalice Well with its garden has been a place of peace and harmony, a sacred timeless sanctuary full of symbolism and atmosphere. Not surpisingly it has a strong elemental quality about it, particularly when one considers that originally, before it was in any way enclosed, this spot would have simply been the home of the running water of a spring.

Mystics describe this little valley as a thousand-petalled lotus whose water-energy spreads out over Glastonbury, and they see the water as magnetised by the polarised energies of the Tor and Chalice Hill. Visitors to the Well have been astonished by the photographs they have taken here, for many of them, when developed, have revealed inexplicable shafts of light.

No visit to Glastonbury is complete without a taste of the delicious waters from Chalice Well: it can be collected at any time from a spout coming directly through the garden wall into Well House Lane.

Entrance in Wellhouse Lane

THE WHITE SPRING

If you walk up Well House Lane, you will notice on the right side of the road, almost opposite the spout of water coming through from Chalice Well Gardens, a grotto looking like an ancient pagan shrine. This houses what has become known as the White Spring. It owes its name to the accretions of white calcite formed on the exposed limestone and branches which used to be submerged in the water.

Originally the grotto was overhung with trees and all kinds of moisture-loving vegetation. Water oozed through and down the stone walls. It was in fact used as a reservoir in the 1870s and then became derelict for decades. In the 1980s the site was bought, and efforts are being made to revive it as one of the locations in the mythology of Glastonbury Tor.

The water of the White Spring has very little iron content and an irregular rate of flow, quite unlike the Chalice Well water. The flow can vary from 500 to over 50,000 gallons a day. The source of the water is unknown. All that is known is that it must pass through this area of Somerset limestone beds before it is pushed up below Glastonbury Tor. There it is apparently diverted by the hard Midford sandstone of the summit and flows laterally through the softer layers of blue limestone and marl to emerge at the White Spring site.

Old photographs of this area show several overgrown small recesses into the hillside which would have indeed been the sites of springs of water. The Bristol Waterworks Company made what is called a 'heading' to cap the underground springs and a brick-lined tunnel stretching about fifty feet into the hill, called a 'collapsed chamber' was discovered. This is, however, comparatively new and does not stretch back into ancient times.

Nevertheless, modern Druids have always seen this site as the entrance to an ancient Druid cave. Others are convinced this spot marks the entrance to the pagan Underworld, the Celtic Annwn, and that Gwyn ap Nudd, Lord of the Underworld and King of Faery, resided here. There are all kinds of tales about the symbolism of the colours Red and White: the red of Chalice Well water and the white of the White Spring. Psychics tend to feel this area at the foot of the Tor as distinctly dark. One could well imagine this spot as an entrance to the pagan Annwn, and visitors are now bringing offerings and tying ribbons here, believing it to be a potent shrine.

Certainly the site of the White Spring reflects a tremendous revival of interest in springs and holy wells which, in ancient times, were revered as sacred. But whereas we have mentions of the Chalice Well tracing it back into the distant past, so far we have only speculation on the White Spring. However, it makes an interesting stopoff on your journey up or down the Tor. Refreshments can be bought, and many of the wilder Glastonbury specimens of humanity can be seen.

The ancient oaks at Wick

GOG AND MAGOG

One of the most beautiful walks around Glastonbury leads to the ancient "Oaks of Avalon" which can be reached by a National Trust footpath from Wick Hollow, over the vale called Paradise and then to the foot of Stonedown. Gog and Magog, with their gnarled shapes and strange faces, are all that remains of what was once an avenue of oaks leading towards the Tor. This avenue was cut down around 1906 to clear the ground of a farm. An eyewitness to this event remembered one of the oaks being eleven feet in diameter and more than two thousand season-rings being counted.

Prehistory

The worship of trees played a very important part in the religious history of the Aryan race who lived in the primeval forests of central Europe. Just imagine the vastness of a forest which took two months to cross, as Caesar described the Hercynian forest in Germany. In Britain forests covered the whole of the southeast, stretching westward to join more forest from Hampshire to Devon.

As far as we know, the most ancient Goddess shrines consisted of a sacred fire perpetually burning in a sacred grove of oaks and fed by oak twigs (at Nemi, for example). All sacred trees were originally dedicated to the Great Mother.

To the Druids among the Celts of Gaul, nothing was more sacred than the mistletoe and the oak on which it grew. Their rites were performed with oak leaves and their sanctuaries were always among groves of oak. Indeed the name Druid is supposed to mean 'oak-men'. Oak trees were regarded as a source of fertility to the land and fecundity to cattle and probably much more besides, considering the number of sacred festivals and celebrations involving the oak in ancient times.

To the ancient Greeks Zeus was the great god of oak, thunder and rain; to the ancient Italian kings the oak was sacred to Jupiter. In fact these gods usurped the oak from Diana, to whom it originally belonged, and Dagda, the chief of the Irish gods, took the oak from Danu, the Celtic goddess. According to Virgil, the oak is the tree of endurance and triumph. Because its roots are said to extend as deep underground as its branches rise in the air, it is symbolic of one who rules above, as below.

The old midsummer fire celebrations were always fuelled with oak. The fire of Vesta in Rome was fed with oak, and many authorities including Caesar concur that sacrifices by fire were practised systematically by the Celts. According to Frazer's *Golden Bough*, wicker-work giants or colossal giants of wood and leaves were made by the Druidic Celts, wrong-doers were put inside and the images then set alight. Although such cruel practices are usually assumed to have originated in very early times, modern-day Goddess-worshippers suggest they date only from the time when male gods replaced the Goddess. The festival would end with funeral feasts in the oak-king's honour to ensure a good harvest and to bring fertility to the crops. The medieval European equivalents of these ancient fire festivals were attempts to break the power of witchcraft. Even though the extent of witch-burning in the Middle Ages reached serious proportions, the practice of human sacrifices by burning probably stemmed from the Celtic Druids, who would thus have been able to enforce their power of priesthood over the local population.

History

According to Geoffrey of Monmouth, when Brutus came to Britain around 1130 BC, he and his people drove the 'Giants' into mountain caves. Goemagot (or Gogmagog), a monster said to be twelve cubits high who lived in the West Country and could pull up an oak tree in one go, was pursued and killed by one of the companions of Brutus. Brutus was said to be the descendant of Aeneas of Troy and the first of the British kings. In the *Receuill des Histoires de Troye* he and his companions brought two giants called Gog and Magog with them, hence the old statues of the same name in the Guildhall, London.

The name Magog turns up again in *The History of the Britons* (796 AD) where Nennius calls Magog the second son of Japhet, the son of Noah. And in Ezekiel 38 and 39 as well as Revelation 20, Gog and Magog are said to be evil powers. Lionel Smithett Lewis, vicar of Glastonbury in the 1920s, says in his book *St Joseph of Arimathea at Glastonbury* that Gog could be a short version of Gomer: "Gomer, from whom came the Gomeri or Cwmri (Cymri = Welsh) the forefathers of the British, who was the eldest-born of Japhet. It was because the Cymri were the eldest-born of the tribes of Japhet that the Arch-Druid was found on this Island, and not on the Continent."

Many sacred sites in Britain and Europe have a grove of yews or oaks nearby. The Celtic Druids could have used this oak grove as a sanctuary and the ancient avenue of oak trees as a processional path to the Tor to conduct their ceremonies. The rituals of Goddess-worship no longer survive intact, but as with so many pagan festivals, we can assume that many of their symbolic features were transferred to Druidic and Christian rituals. These are all we have left.

Modern Druids used to meet at Glastonbury every year for the Beltane festival, and Gog and Magog was the chosen site for a ceremony that included threading a maze and leaping over the flames of a bonfire. The gnarled branches and hollow insides of the trees used to be wonderful for climbing and hiding in. Picnics were held there to celebrate the tree spirits. Now these venerable trees are under a conservation order—which is probably just as well. But it is sad that Gog and Magog are now fenced in with barbed wire which prevents us from feeling and touching them.

Magog in midwinter

Mary Caine's version of Katherine Maltwood's Temple of the Stars

THE GLASTONBURY ZODIAC

Many Glastonbury enthusiasts have regarded the zodiac as the key to all the myths associated with this place. Some would go further and suggest that the Glastonbury zodiac is the most important discovery in that it is the story of creation. Indeed, it is a fascinating thought-provoking phenomenon but, like so much of our dim and distant past, it is wide open to interpretation.

In 1935 Katherine Maltwood announced her discovery of the Glastonbury zodiac. She had been asked to do illustrations for the medieval romance, *The High History of the Holy Grail*, reputedly written at Glastonbury Abbey, and as she researched her material, she found that the castles and adventures of the knights of the Round Table corresponded to places in the Vale of Avalon. As she read about the knights' encounters with dragons, lions, giants and others, then traced on the map the places where these adventures took place, she began to notice the outline of a huge lion delineated by the river Cary and an ancient road.

Other figures slowly revealed themselves, delineated by streams, tracks and boundaries, and before long she had discovered twelve signs of the zodiac in their correct order with the thirteenth figure— the great dog of Langport—outside the circle to the southwest, guarding the winter signs to the north and the summer signs to the south. She called her discovery the *Temple of the Stars* because, placing a map of the stars over the circle of effigies, the stars and their respective constellations corresponded.

Associations with the zodiac

There is a wealth of symbolism in these giant figures and, in fact, the zodiac can represent all things to all people. The word zodiac means simply the way or path which the sun appears to follow among the stars in the course of a year. However, it can also be regarded as the twelve steps in the story of creation or the twelve steps to awareness and perfection as found in *The Labours of Hercules*. Yet again it can mean the search for knowledge and enlightenment as told in the stories and legends of the Holy Grail. Each quest can be seen as an initiation. And indeed according to the Norman *Quest for the Holy Grail*, King Arthur's Round Table means "the round world and round canopy of the planets and the elements in the firmament, where are to be seen the stars and many other things."

The number twelve is certainly worth noting as, apart from the well-known twelve tribes of Israel, there are numerous examples of twelve-tribe societies throughout the ancient world. These nomadic twelve tribes would move around in a twelve-monthly cycle reflecting the procession of the sun through the zodiac. In Celtic societies King

Arthur took on the role of the sun and as he progressed through the twelve signs of the zodiac, King Arthur's court would preside over meetings, festivals and judgments. We can well imagine this Arthurian mythic cycle taking place around the Twelve Hides of Glastonbury for there is such a wealth of Arthurian lore and legend in the landscape.

The Signs in the landscape

Aries

This figure is two miles long. It is a hornless lamb with its head turning back and outlined by the town of Street with its feet tucked underneath. Just as Aries is the first sign of the zodiac, the sign of spring, so Gawain is the first knight in Arthurian legend. His story is that of youthful folly, being thrown out of the Grail Castle for failing to ask or understand its meaning until he is older and wiser. In *The Labours of Hercules* this sign sees Hercules attempting the capture of the man-eating mares. It is the first step in the circle of experience.

Taurus

Only the bull's head and forefoot are delineated here in a smaller figure a mile long. The outlines are very clearly made by ancient roads. The Pleiades constellation falls on the top of Collard Hill, the bull's collar; Hood Monument is a third horn on the bull's head, and coiled earthworks make up his ear. In Arthurian legend, Taurus could be Sir Ector, young Arthur's foster-father, for Taurus can be regarded as the solid provider of shelter. In *The Labours of Hercules* Taurus sees Hercules capture the Cretan Bull.

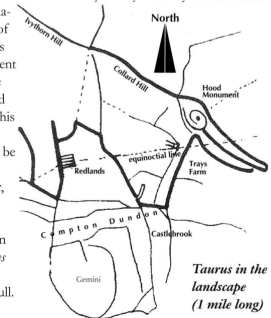

Taurus in the landscape (1 mile long)

Gemini

Here the large head of a child or baby is shown, a mile and a half long, made up by the round steep fort of Dundon Hill. The figure's chest is Lollover Hill and the stars of Pollux, Castor's twin brother, fall on his upraised arm while Orion's stars fall on his body. Orion was once the most famous of giants representing the sun in the west. Here his Arthurian counterpart would be Arthur's son Lohot who had a habit of falling asleep on the bodies of giants he had slain. In *The Labours of Hercules* Gemini is the gathering of the Golden Apples of the Hesperides.

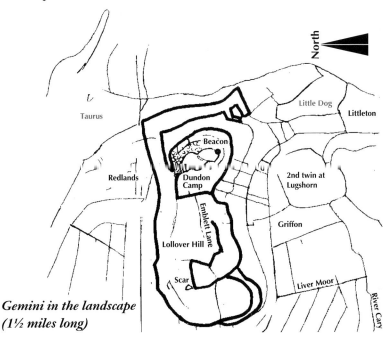

Gemini in the landscape (1½ miles long)

Cancer

Unlike all the other effigies, this figure is inanimate: its outlines are completely straight and made by water dykes. It is the shape of a ship with the Gemini child rising out of it. Three miles long in all, the main mast of the ship is over a mile. Its shape comes from the constellation Argo Navis; the stars of the hare Lepus fall upon it and, interestingly, to the Ancient Egyptians, Lepus was the name of Osiris' funeral barge. In Arthurian legend the ship is King Solomon's—made to last forever until the perfect knight should come. In *The Labours of Hercules* Cancer is the story of the capture of the doe or hind, the doe who was sacred to Artemis the goddess of the Moon, but who was also claimed by Diana, Huntress of the Heavens.

Leo

This is a three-mile-long heraldic lion near Somerton, an ancient capital of Wessex. The lion's underside is outlined by the River Cary and its mane is Copley Woods. In Arthurian myth, Lancelot—the Summer Sun—symbolises Leo. The Celts called the winter solstice Alban Arthan and therefore it can be said that the Sun of Winter (Arthur) was hunting the Sun of Summer (Lancelot). Arthur imprisons Lancelot but has to let him out in due season.

Because of its large size, Leo includes the whole constellation of Cancer in its neck as well as Castor and Pollux from Gemini. The head of the Hydra is within its body and Leo's Royal Star Regulus is there too. In *The Labours of Hercules* Leo is represented by the slaying of the Nemean Lion.

Virgo

The figure here is of an old crone four miles long, one of the aspects of the Goddess. Her profile is outlined by the River Cary and she stands on Wheathill suggesting the harvest Goddess who holds wheat in her hand. In fact, the object in her hand at Stickle Bridge is three-cornered and could be either a wheatsheaf, a broomstick or a trident. In *The High History of the Holy Grail* Virgo is the Damsel, Sir Perceval's sister, called Dindrain as well according to Katherine Maltwood. But to Mary Caine, author of *The Glastonbury Zodiac*, she is also Guinevere because of the River Cam, Camel Hill, West Camel and Queen Camel nearby, and because the figure leans towards Leo, who is Lancelot. In *The Labours of Hercules* Virgo sees Hercules seizing the Girdle of Hippolyte.

Libra

Here at Barton St David is the shape of a dove a mile and a half long. Unlike the Roman symbol for Libra of the scales, the dove represents mercy and pure spirit in many ancient mythologies. Libra's stars do not correspond here. Instead, the largest constellation of all, the Plough, falls on this figure. In Arthurian legend the dove flies across the hall of the Grail Castle, preceding the grail procession and lighting up the scene like a supernatural messenger. In Libra Hercules captures the Erymanthian Boar.

Scorpio

The tail is the most convincing part of this effigy with its sting at West Lydford, very close to Arthur's head at Catsham. Scorpio has four legs on either side at Four Foot Farm and Bridgefoot Bridge. Libra's stars fall on Scorpio's claw, the stars of Lupus and Serpens are within the figure, the Royal Star Antares and five other Scorpio stars mark the centre of its body along the Fosse Way. In *The High History of the Holy Grail* Scorpio is the dead hermit Callixtus whose wasted life is weighed against him by quarrelling demons and angels. The angels win by a hair's breadth. Scorpio could also be Mordred in Arthurian lore, for the Persians used to call the month of November *Mordad*. Destroying the Lernaean Hydra is the story of Scorpio in *The Labours of Hercules*.

Sagittarius

Here is the five-mile-long figure of King Arthur on his horse. His head is at Catsham, his outstretched arm at Baltonsborough, and his knee at Ponter's Ball. The horse is shaped by the Pennard Hills with Arthur's Bridge by its tail. Almost the whole constellation of Hercules corresponds with this effigy while all the stars of Lyra fall on his back. The figure can be seen as the archer Sagittarius with arms outstretched drawing a bow. Killing the Stymphalian Birds is the Sagittarius episode for Hercules.

In Malory's *Morte d'Arthur* there is a description which could fit the Arthur/Sagittarius effigy, for Capricorn, Scorpio and the Whale are all threatening him:

> King Arthur dreamed a wonderful dream ... it seemed he sat upon a chaflet in a chair ... fast to a wheel, and thereupon he sat in the richest cloth of gold that might be made; and the King thought there was under him, far from him, a hideous deep black water, and therein were all manner of serpents and worms and wild beasts, foul and horrible, and suddenly the king thought the wheel turned upside down, and he fell among the serpents, and every beast took him by a limb.

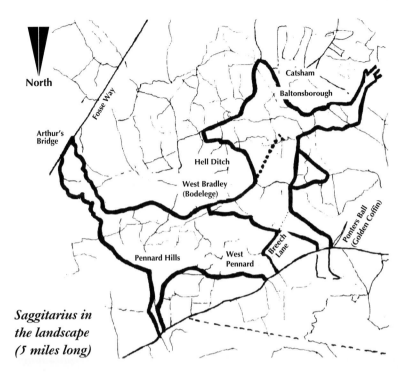

*Saggitarius in
the landscape
(5 miles long)*

Capricorn

Here are the perfect outlines of a goat three and a half miles across.
The goat's back is traced by the road from Glastonbury to Shepton
Mallet, and its horn is at the earthwork of Ponter's Ball (this horn is
known locally as the Golden Coffin), making it more like a unicorn.
The lion-and-unicorn symbolism fits well here because the unicorn's
figure points southwest to the lion's paw in Leo. In *The High History of
the Holy Grail* Capricorn is the King of Castle Mortal who makes war
with King Fisherman, but the knight Perceval finally gets rid of him.
In *The Labours of Hercules* Capricorn is the slaying of Cerberus,
Guardian of Hades.

Aquarius

One and a half miles across in Glastonbury itself, Aquarius is
represented by the figure of the phoenix or eagle with wings spread
out. The wings, body and head are completely outlined by hills with
the Tor on the bird's head. Chalice Well is at the end of its beak—
perfect Aquarian symbolism for the water-carrier. In sun-worship

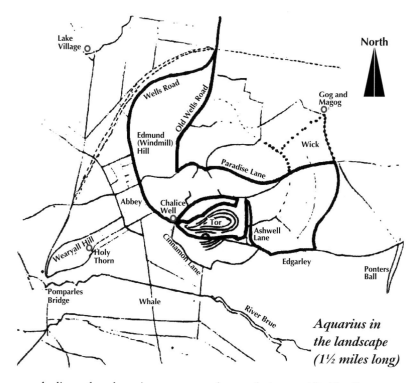

Aquarius in the landscape (1½ miles long)

symbolism, the phoenix represents the sun being purified by fire at sunset and rising out of the ashes of the night. The Tor's spiral maze delineates the throat of the bird, which turns towards the Chalice Spring's regenerative powers. Chalice Hill forms part of the body and Glastonbury Abbey is on its tail. Sadal Melik, Skat, and several other stars of Aquarius correspond with the wings, and Markab from Pegasus falls by its crest.

In *The High History of the Holy Grail* Perceval is the sun in the first quarter of the year, and his title *Par-lui-fet* means "he who has made himself", which is just like the phoenix who remakes itself and is resurrected. In *The Labours of Hercules* Aquarius sees Hercules cleansing the Augean Stables.

Pisces

Here are the effigies of two fishes and a whale. One fish is Wearyall Hill; the other is in the town of Street. The whale extends from Hulk Moor west of Pomparles Bridge along the River Brue to close to Wallyer's Bridge. In the mythology of sun worship, a fish was supposed to swallow the sun as it sank down into the sea—an appropriate image for the lake villagers of Glastonbury and Meare.

In *The High History of the Holy Grail* the Castle of the Whale episode tells of the whale with a serpent's head. Perceval rows down the river, finds the snake's head (according to Katherine Maltwood, the head is in the exact centre of the zodiac at Parkwood) and, piercing the animal's throat, pulls out the key with which to release the prisoner of the Whale Castle. The stars of Pisces correspond with the tail of the whale, one of the fishes, and the road connecting them. Pisces is represented by the capture of the Red Cattle of Geryon in *The Labours of Hercules*.

The Thirteenth Giant

This is a five-mile-long figure of a dog standing outside the zodiac. It is larger than life and cannot be ignored. It is known as the Great Dog of Langport and is referred to in the old Somerset Wassail song:

> *The Girt Dog of Langport has burnt his long tail*
> *And this is the night we go singing wassail.*

Immediately southwest of the zodiac circle, the figure is like the Egyptian dog Anubis, Guardian of the Underworld. Here the dog could be said to be guarding the zodiac. Its tail is appropriately at a place called Wagg, and the bright Dog Star of Canis Major—Sirius—falls on the dog's nose. Just by its nose is the hill at Athelney, which is one of the line of hills making up the longest alignment of prehistoric sites in southern England. In *The High History of the Holy Grail* the dog is female. She is the questing beast who gives birth to twelve hounds who tear her with their teeth "but no power had they to devour her flesh." Hecate, the goddess of the crossroads and of witches, was accompanied by a dog.

According to Katherine Maltwood, who discovered the Glastonbury zodiac, it could have been the Sumerians (who might have given their name to Somerset) who designed it around five thousand years ago. Others see the zodiac as the magnetic action of the sun, moon and stars printed on the sensitive Glastonbury landscape long before astrology was even thought of.

However we see this strange phenomenon, as we enquire into its origins, the figures and shapes give us meaning. Made up as they are of historical and cultural archetypes, they help us relate to abstract principles and cosmic harmonics, even if this is on a purely subliminal level. Without doubt we owe a tremendous debt to Katherine Maltwood for making us aware of how the ancient world related to the landscape and the stars; in rediscovering their geomantic works today, once again we find the landscape speaks to us.

If your appetite has been whetted and you cannot afford to hire a helicopter or take lessons in levitation, you can experience the Glastonbury zodiac by walking around it. It will be a long trek, so be sure to take a map.

THE GEORGE & PILGRIMS HOTEL

In the days when Glastonbury Abbey was internationally famous for its wealth, architectural beauty and reputation as an important centre of learning, large numbers of visitors and pilgrims would flock to Glastonbury. Visitors were admitted to the Abbey for varying lengths of stay, dictated by certain rules and free of charge. But the numbers increased so dramatically that a house for paying guests was erected outside the Abbey walls, still under the supervision of an Abbey official.

This was called The George or The Pilgrims' Inn and is now the hotel at the bottom of the High Street, below the Tribunal and just by the Market Cross. The building appears to date from around 1475, the time when John Selwood was abbot (1456–1493). It is a highly ornamented building with an embattled parapet surmounted at each end by an octagonal turret rising from the base of the building. The mullioned windows were inserted later and over the gateway there were three shields, one of the St George's Cross, the central one of the Arms of Edward IV, and the third of unknown origin.

At one time the building was decorated with figures of the twelve Caesars and a mutilated figure of charity. There was also supposed to be a subterranean passage leading from the cellar of the inn to the Abbey. Inside are old timber beams adorned with carved angels and guarded by deathmasks of monks. There are Dutch tiles from more than 200 years ago and Glastonbury chairs modelled on the original medieval design.

If you choose to stay at the George and Pilgrims Hotel, you may spend the night in The Nun's Cell, The Confessional, or rooms named after Abbot Beere or Henry VIII. Beware things that go bump in the night!

Ancient building houses Tourist Information Centre

THE TRIBUNAL

The Tribunal until recently was thought to be the courthouse of Glastonbury where the abbot sat in judgment—in the Middle Ages he had complete jurisdiction over the Twelve Hides, a large area surrounding the Abbey. It is on the left side of Glastonbury High Street as you walk upwards from the Market Cross. The name Tribunal was given to this fifteenth-century building in 1791, although it is now considered to be a late-medieval town house, "perhaps that of a rich merchant, lawyer or townsman". A 1716 document mentions "a small old building of stone called Beere's Hospital". If this in fact

refers to the Tribunal building, it would have been used in Abbot
Beere's time (1493–1503) as a hospice or inn. There seems to be some
confusion; documentary records hardly exist. But in the 18th century
the building may have been used as "a commercial school for young
gentlemen".

Perhaps the origin of the building's stone facade is of most
interest. The antiquarian William Stukeley published an engraving
dated 1712 showing the Abbot's Lodgings behind the Kitchen in the
Abbey grounds. The Lodgings disappeared within that decade; its
stone bay-window and arched doorways look suspiciously similar to
the present Tribunal facade. Could it have been imported from the
ruins of the Abbey? The framed ceiling over the front room and
some of the stone doorways seem to have survived from the 15th
century. The wooden door with heavy strap hinges and iron studs is
original, and above the door are two square panels: one bearing the
Tudor royal arms surmounted by a crown with a dragon and lion as
supporters, the other containing a Tudor rose.

The kitchen block at the back was added later, close to the well
in the courtyard.

Since 1992 the Tribunal building has been managed by
Glastonbury Tribunal Ltd under licence from English Heritage, with
the aim of providing a Tourist Information Centre and housing the
Glastonbury Lake Village Museum—which is well worth a visit. This
museum, located upstairs, is set out clearly and concisely. The history
is fully described, reconstructions and pictures show what the Lake
Village (see page 35) would have looked like, and all the finds from the
site, including jewellery, tools and pottery, are on display.

THE CHURCH OF SAINT JOHN BAPTIST

The finest view of St John's Church in Glastonbury High Street is obtained from a distance, from one of the surrounding hills and when the sun is shining. The tower, 134½ feet high, is the third-tallest parish church tower in Somerset and it rises magnificently out of the town especially when glimpsed from Wearyall Hill, Chalice Hill or the Tor. It is said that the tower was built by Abbot Selwood in 1475—it is much more richly decorated than the rest of the church. The whole tower is encased in Doulting ashlar, which reflects the light. It is generally regarded as one of the finest examples of a Norman tower.

From Saxon times, Glastonbury Abbey had complete jurisdiction over the Church of St John Baptist as well as over seven other local churches. There is no information to be found on the original Saxon church, although we know that by 1203 there was a Norman church with a central tower which would have had the same sort of ground plan as the present structure. Originally the parishioners would have worshipped in the Abbey church, which was the custom in all the early Benedictine houses. However, parishioners had to pay a rent of six shillings and ninepence to the Abbey, and Pope Honorius III stated in 1225 that revenues from the church were appropriated to help the Abbey's building fund after the fire of 1184.

The present building was completed by the end of the fifteenth century; rebuilding and refurnishing went on all through the century, according to churchwardens' accounts dating from 1366 onwards. Inside are two tall arcades of seven bays with clerestory windows above. Aisle windows are early fifteenth century but those of the clerestory are later. The tower arch is panelled and the roof fan-vaulted. From the inside it is obvious that originally the church was cruciform, with the tower rising at the end of the nave, and transepts extending right and left. At the east end is an altar tomb of John Attewell (1472) and one of Joan Attewell (1485)—both benefactors of the church. On the wall over the north tomb is an ivory crucifix said to have been in the possession of Judge Jeffries and King George IV.

St George's Chapel, where the holy sacrament is reserved, is in the south transept with the alabaster tomb of John Cammell, who died in 1487. The south window of the sanctuary depicts an archbishop and the shield adopted by Abbot Beere in fifteenth century glass—a cross and two cruets—a clear illustration of the Holy Blood which Joseph of Arimathea caught from the wounds of Christ on the cross and brought to England. The green cross with shoots is an allusion to the Holy Thorn. There is also a striking stained-glass window of Joseph of Arimathea in St John's Church, well worth seeing, and an early Glastonbury chair, once owned by Horace Walpole.

Today, Holy Communion is on Sundays at 8am and at 9:30 (with music and laying-on-of-hands for healing) and at various weekday times. Two Sundays monthly have a more free-form "Six O'Clock Service".

SAINT BENEDICT'S CHURCH

This church in Benedict Street at the lower end of the town, and meaningfully situated in line with the Abbey church, is dedicated to St Benignus. According to the Glastonbury chroniclers, he was a disciple of St Patrick who followed him to Glastonbury from Ireland and lived as a hermit at Meare. According to Irish tradition, Benignus was baptized by St Patrick, who predicted that he would become his heir.

There are many legends about St Benignus but we do know that his relics were moved with great ceremony from Meare to Glastonbury in 1091. However, Irish pilgrims may have confused the name Benignus with Beonna, a local holy man from Meare—and then the name was further confused with St Benedict, whose Rule governed the Abbey since St Dunstan's time. Apparently, so many miracles occurred along the route, including a column of light streaming down on the chapel at Meare and a rainbow over the Abbey, that a church was built on the site and dedicated to him. This was replaced by the present St Benedict's Church at the turn of the sixteenth century; his relics, however, were put next to St Patrick's and St Indract's in a shrine at the High Altar at Glastonbury Abbey. William of Malmesbury wrote of a cult to St Benignus in a work of his called *Life* in the 1120s, then John of Glastonbury in his *Cronica sive Antiquitates Glastoniensis Ecclesie* around the 1340s resumed the stories.

The present St Benedict's Church has a chancel of earlier date than 1500 and other later additions of the Victorian period. The building is typical of Somerset Perpendicular design with a double arcade of four bays. Perhaps of greatest interest is a set of carved roof corbels that show the legend of St Benignus, the arms of Glastonbury Abbey and the rebus of Abbot Beere.

SAINT MARY'S CHURCH

Overlooking Glastonbury Abbey on the other side of Magdalene Street and on land which formerly made up the Abbot's Park of Wirral, stands the Roman Catholic Church of Saint Mary. Built in 1939, it is regarded by Catholics as the successor to the old wattle church dedicated to Mary, the Mother of Christ, and is seen as the shrine of Our Lady of Glastonbury, having been canonically restored in the name of the Holy See.

A statue of Mary entitled Our Lady St Mary of Glastonbury is to be found in the church. The design was taken from the representation of Mary in a fourteenth-century metal seal of the Abbey, and she is shown crowned, with a veil and mantle, holding the baby Jesus in one arm and a sprig of blossom in the other. The original Abbey seal showed St Catherine of Alexandria with a wheel, Mary in the middle with babe and blossom, and St Margaret with a dragon. The inscription reads: "The Holy Mother of Christ is witness to this writing—Glaston." On the other side are St Patrick, St Dunstan and St Benignus with the inscription: "The three bishops confirm these things."

Glastonbury's Catholic church also possesses a tapestry woven in 1965 and depicting the Glastonbury legends and history. It was designed by Brother Louis Barlow of the Benedictine abbey at Prinknash, Gloucestershire. Against a background of the Abbey and St Michael's tower on the Tor are the following Glastonbury-related figures: Joseph of Arimathea with his blossoming staff and Holy Grail, Saints David, Patrick, Brigid, Dunstan, Abbot Richard Beere, Abbot Richard Whiting and his assistant martyred monks John Thorne and Roger James.

The cult of Mary

You will remember from previous chapters that Mary, the Mother of Christ, figured prominently at the very beginning of Christian Glastonbury. The old wattle church, said to be the first church in England, was dedicated to her (see page 43). It is perhaps appropriate, therefore, to attempt a brief descriptive background to her cult here, under the heading of Glastonbury's Catholic Church—for it is among Catholics that her mystique and divinity survive.

The most ancient religion we know of was that of the Great Goddess who was known variously as Queen of Heaven, Mother of all Things, Mighty Mother, the Great Deep, the Celestial Abyss, the All-Creative, Mystery of the Heavens, Moon Mother, Earth Mother and She-who-gives-Life-to-the-Dead. Gradually, however, male consorts began to appear alongside the Goddess and this marked the waning of her power. These male dependents were then transmuted into brothers or lovers and came at length to be seen as her equal. The male takeover was completed by the second millennium BC, when the Goddess was demoted to numerous lesser goddesses, becoming the

Neolithic Goddess from Hluboke Masuvky, Moravia,Czech Republic

Our Lady of Glastonbury statuette in St Mary's Catholic Church

"daughters of Zeus" or figures simply of male desire. The total and complete denigration of the female deity, however, can be traced to the cult of the Hebrew God Yahweh, for here the Mother of All became the trouble-maker Eve who, with her serpent, is actually made responsible for the downfall of humanity.

The goddess Isis is classically represented enthroned, breast-feeding her divine son—an image which was the model for the Madonna-and-Child paintings and sculptures so often thought of as solely Christian. Isis too is Maiden, Mother, and Bride, and both Isis and Mary voyage across the sky in the crescent moon.

Another phenomenon linking devotion to Mary with Goddess worship is in her association with particular places. Mary is worshipped all over the Catholic world as "Our Lady of" a particular shrine, just as the pagan Goddess was celebrated on hills or by springs or wells. But modern-day Goddess worshippers and new pagans cannot relate to the Virgin Mary as they can to the many-faceted Goddess of old. To them Mary's image is an emasculation—usually subservient to her Son. Geoffrey Ashe, author of many books on myth and legend including *The Virgin*, a fascinating inquiry into the cult of Mary, takes another view:

> Mary in her medieval cult was by no means meek and mild or subservient to her Son. It was popularly supposed that as Queen of Heaven she was a sort of Queen-Mother and *he* would do anything *she* asked him to—a good reason for cultivating her favour. Something of this attitude survived into the 20th century though the Second Vatican Council tried to soft-pedal Mariolatry. If the solar phenomenon at Fatima in 1917, which threw a huge crowd into a panic, was (as believers affirmed) Mary's doing, it hardly suggested meekness and mildness.

THE ALMSHOUSES

Near St Mary's Church in Magdalene Street is an alleyway leading to a
row of old almshouses with a small chapel. The Almshouses may
have been founded as early as 1264 as "the gift and foundation of the
Abbots of Glaston". They housed up to ten poor men before 1322.
After the Dissolution they were known as the Royal Hospital,
financed by grants from the Crown.

Elements of the chapel date to the thirteenth and fifteenth
centuries, although the present buildings were begun in the fifteenth
century. The bellcote depicts St Margaret, which suggests that the

hospital could have been for sick women rather than for men.

There were originally two rows of almshouses, with only a narrow gangway, the present path, between them. In 1958 one row was demolished and the remaining row and the chapel repaired. Mendip District Council carried out further refurbishments in 1996.

Today, the Almshouses and chapel are leased by the Quest Community, a local Christian group formed in 1993, inspired by the Iona Community in Scotland, with the aim of caring for pilgrims to Glastonbury. Informal prayers are held in the chapel most days at noon, and the Almshouses are used for crafts, library and counselling. The community also sets up The Coracle, for counselling and prayer, every year at the Glastonbury Festival at Pilton.

The Celtic Wheel of the Year

ANCIENT FESTIVALS

To ancient nomadic peoples and the Celts, time was not a linear process. Instead, they saw the year as a cyclic journey through the seasons with gatherings and festivals deeply interwoven with their mythology. These festivals were intrinsically linked with night and day, sun and moon, and their calendar was based on the astronomical divisions of the year into solstices and equinoxes. The Celts also used a midpoint between the solstices and equinoxes called the cross-quarters. These are Samhain, Imbolc, Beltane and Lughnasa.

Eight festivals made up the Celtic year: four quarter-days and four solar divisions (two solstices and two equinoxes). At least from Celtic times, these festivals were celebrated with fires, games and ancient rites and rituals.

All these festivals are celebrated in one way or another in Glastonbury today. The high place or sacred hilltop for the evening vigil is Glastonbury Tor; daytime rituals and events are held either in the Assembly Rooms or in a room belonging to the Isle of Avalon Foundation. But, as usual in Glastonbury, people tend to do their own thing depending on their predilection for a particular sacred site.

June 21—Summer solstice

Midsummer fires were lit at crossroads and on hilltops on solstice eve, and a vigil was kept till sunrise. During the day a burning wheel was rolled down a hill to represent the sun's course in the sky as its annual decline begins. The sun is at its furthest north giving us the most daylight hours of a year; the sun's power is at its peak. But the night hours now begin to increase. This is the time to express our hopes and intentions, to celebrate the summer months.

August 1—Lughnasa or Lammas

This festival celebrated the beginning of harvest-time or the day of 'first fruits'. As an assurance that the sun would retain its power until the harvest was complete, the Celts celebrated a ritual marriage on this day between Lugh, the sun, and Eire, the earth. This cosmic mating was vital to the maintenance of harmony and abundance. Lugh, the Celtic god of Light, would bury his foster mother Tailltiu beneath a great mound in Ireland at Lammas/Lughnasa, so that she would take care of the falling seeds and make sure they germinated well in winter. This day would be marked with a gathering often taking place beside a lake, holy well or at the top of a sacred hill or mountain. This is the time when green turns to gold; it is nature's peak that we celebrate, knowing it is almost over.

September 21—Autumn equinox

This is the main harvest-time and the midpoint of autumn. Day and night are of equal length but daylight hours are steadily diminishing. The eve of this festival, like all other festivals, was regarded as the magical spiritual time, whereas the daylight hours would be spent in gatherings and celebrations. This is a festival of thanksgiving for the abundance of the harvest, a time to stop and adjust to the transition to the winter season.

October 31—Samhain

This is the point in the cycle of our seasons when the veil between dimensions is lifted and the underworld becomes more visible. This is twilight-zone time when the world of our physical reality and the world of spirit come together. This festival has become our Halloween with people dressing up as ghosts and witches. In Irish mythology, this is when the faery mounds open up and the other 'side' can be glimpsed. In ancient times the costumes worn at Samhain were the horns and skins of game animals, worn to show respect for the lives given for the tribe to survive. Rituals were enacted at burial mounds to connect with the dead; shamanic journeys were undertaken to gain healing powers or knowledge of the underworld, and the old year was burned in effigy. It is a time to honour death as part of life, and see omens and auguries for the coming year.

December 21—Winter solstice

The sun has journeyed to its furthest south, hence the least daylight hours. This is the time of the sun's death and rebirth: the sun was seen withdrawing into a cave or beneath the earth and had to be lured out by rites and rituals. Purging the winter demons who were keeping the sun prisoner was one form of ancient ritual. In some mythologies the sun dies at winter solstice and is reborn as a young deity who grows to adulthood during the course of the year, climaxing at summer solstice. Both the summer and winter solstices were celebrated universally in all cultures, for only at these times the sun seems to rise from the same place for three or four days. It appears to 'stop' when it reaches the furthest point of its journey north or south. Hence the term solstice from the Latin *solsistit* meaning 'the sun is made to stand still'.

February 1—Imbolc

In ancient Britain this festival was known as Oimelc and later Brigantia to celebrate the goddess Bridget (Brighde, Brigid or Brigit), a deity of maidens and poetry, healing and smiths. When Bridget was christianised, this became St Brigid's Day, and if a ribbon or cloth was exposed in a sacred place, it became endowed with healing powers. A tradition that involves making Brighde dolls for good luck survives to this day, but traditionally this is a pastoral festival celebrating the ewes' coming into milk. On the eve of Imbolc, the Old Crone goddess of winter, the Cailleach, drinks from the sacred well and is transformed into the virgin Bridget. Candlemas on February 2 is celebrated by the Catholic Church as the purification of the Virgin Mary, and torches and candles are lit at midnight. This is a time of transformation from winter to spring, a time for purifying the old and planting new ideas.

March 21—Spring equinox

This is the moment when the sun crosses the Equator, days and nights are of equal length, but sunlight is increasing. The sun has been rescued from her cave prison and light can now triumph over darkness. A number of pagan traditions celebrating the sun's return have been moved from Midsummer and May Day to what is now Easter. Among the pagan Slavs a red egg and a round loaf represented the sun and were taken to a high place where a rite of choral ring-dances took place. The main singer would turn towards the east holding the sun symbols and sing of the destruction of winter and the coming of spring. This is a festival of awakening and germination of seeds. Growth is on its way.

May 1—Beltane

Celebrating the return of the sun's warmth and the renewal of nature, Beltane comes from the Irish word *teine*, meaning solar fire. The Celtic festival of Beltane used to include, on May eve, a ritual sun vigil on a high place where a bonfire would be lit to encourage the sun to come out. The Slavs, like the Celts and other cultures, knew well the tradition of the sun's dance where the rituals of the night turned into anxious waiting for the sun to rise. Once she had risen, the sun would perform a fantastic dance where she would emit coloured sparks, all shades of the rainbow. Our tradition of dancing round the maypole could well have derived from this. This is a time of jumping the fire to purify and bring fertility, a festival for lovers and friends, a time to wear green in the merry month of May.

In all the world mythologies there are variations on the same theme of the sun's journey through the year. One of the few books with original research on the subject is *Eclipse of the Sun: An Investigation of Sun and Moon Myths* by Janet McCrickard.

Worthy Farm, 1997: Year of the Mud

GLASTONBURY CULTURE

As with most things relating to Glastonbury, nothing is quite as it seems. Any attempt here to describe the culture or in any sense pin it down immediately involves sweeping generalisations. The truth remains elusive but for my purposes here, it will have to be subjective.

Regarded as the oldest and holiest of England's spiritual sanctuaries, Glastonbury has always had its pilgrims, the 'hippies' or 'New Age travellers' being merely current versions of the wild specimens of humanity who would have come here in medieval times. History has a way of repeating itself, and just as Glastonbury was a pagan centre before it became a Christian shrine, so now the 'new pagans' have made their home here.

History

The spiritual revival of Glastonbury could be traced to the founding of the Theosophical Society in London in the 1880s. At that time many were influenced by strange yet inspiring tales brought back from India and various corners of the British Empire. It was rumoured that the West lacked all spirituality and was entirely given over to materialism, whereas the East was full of sages and spiritual wisdom. Madame Blavatsky, founder of the Theosophical Society, was inspired by Himalayan Masters, but Dr Anna Kingsford split with her to form the Hermetic Society in order to delve more deeply into the spiritual legacy of the British Isles. Various magical orders with a Western approach followed suit, including the Golden Dawn and a ritualistic group calling itself the Liberal Catholic Church. The poets Tennyson and William Blake began to write about a new spiritual awareness in Britain and socialists as well as new occult groups began to see that our own British myths and legends have much to teach us. Both Blavatsky and Dion Fortune had resurrected the Goddess and the subject of Women's Mysteries, but it was Dion Fortune who finally wrote about Glastonbury as a centre of the Western mystery tradition. (See *The Avalonians* by Patrick Benham for details.)

Along with its reputation as a spiritual centre, Glastonbury was famous throughout the country in the 1920s for its culture. The National Festival Theatre of Music and Drama which came to be known as the 'Glastonbury Festival' began on 5 August 1914 in the Assembly Rooms. It was established by the British composer Rutland Boughton and became the model for art and music festivals such as Bath, Aldburgh, Glyndebourne and subsequent rural festivals. During his stay in Glastonbury, Boughton wrote a series of music dramas based on the Arthurian legends, a choral drama *Bethlehem*, *The Queen of Cornwall* and others including *The Immortal Hour*, which is based on Fiona Macleod's Celtic legend about a faery female and her human lover. Boughton put on performances of these and other works with his Glastonbury Players. In its heyday, patrons, visitors and performers included such cultural giants as Bernard Shaw, Edward

Elgar, Vaughan Williams, Thomas Hardy, D.H. Lawrence, T.E. Lawrence and John Galsworthy.

The Glastonbury Arts Festival was revived in 1996 and saw the performance by local Glastonians of the opera *The Immortal Hour*. Lunchtime concerts at St John's Church, evening concerts in various venues, *son et lumière* in the Abbey grounds, and an arts and crafts exhibition and fair are some of the events now planned to take place yearly at this festival from mid-August to mid-September.

Of course the hippies of the late 1960s had much to do with making Glastonbury famous for a whole new generation. With their nomadic instinct, new-found mysticism, and quest for the meaning of life, they came to Glastonbury and the surrounding countryside, set up communes and craft workshops, and experimented with new ways of living. Then, in 1971, the Glastonbury Fayre was held to celebrate the summer solstice. It was the first of what became an almost annual event in the fields at Pilton five miles away, and the views of Glastonbury Tor and the tales of magic and alternative lifestyles attracted a whole new wave of young people to settle in the area. Glastonbury was the perfect environment with its natural sanctuaries alive with myths and legends and, of course, the magic spell of its sacred landscape.

The present

In the late 1970s there were few outward signs of alternative spiritual aspirations in the town, although spiritual groups like the Winds of Truth had met for years. The Glastonbury Fayre, full-moon meditations and the Gothic Image shop with its Mystical Tours of Glastonbury were the only obvious signs of another kind of thinking in the town. The Assembly Rooms was restored and revived as an arts centre for the community and has more recently been purchased by Friends who run it in a co-operative way. Gog Theatre played a large part in bringing the place to life with their performances. Now it is home to the Gothic Relief Theatre, pantomimes, and all kinds of community activities. A host of New Age shops emerged in the 1980s, alongside a vegetarian cafe and wholefood shop, and the setting up of talks, lectures and workshops on spiritual matters.

Glastonbury is a safe haven for the road-protest movement, who come here for their 'tribal gatherings'. The annual 'Cornference' for crop-circle enthusiasts takes place in the Glastonbury Assembly Rooms, usually in August, and a magazine called *UFO Reality* is put together here. There are Avalon Pipers, didgeridoo players, and all kinds of spinoffs from Ozric Tentacles, the psychedelic rock band. Kangaroo Moon grew out of Glastonbury as did Steve Jolliffe. Spacegoats, Heathens All, and Tofu Love Frogs are local to Glastonbury, as well as younger DJs and mixers. They organise parties and gigs, usually in the Assembly Rooms, and have strong local followings. We also have the powerful sound of the Avalonian Free State Choir.

  The National Federation of Spiritual Healers now has its home here, and anyone can receive healing for a small donation. There are healers of all kinds and counsellors of varying quality, although I would recommend the Natural Health Clinic for its sound approach and sane practitioners. The Isle of Avalon Foundation, to be found in the Glastonbury Experience courtyard off the main High Street, organises lectures and courses, including a yearly Goddess conference taking place at Lammas. The Library of Avalon is to be found here, and it is worth taking a look at its ever-expanding collection of mythological and esoteric titles. The Bridget Chapel, also in this courtyard, is a quiet place to say a prayer. The Christian community is very active and includes the Quest Community; there is an Orthodox shop, and all kinds of Eastern religions have followers here.

  On the last Saturday in June every year Glastonbury is host to the Anglican pilgrimage when clergy from all over England gather with their congregations to process, with hymns and incense, down the High Street and take communion at the high altar of Glastonbury Abbey—the oldest church. The Catholic Church meets here the next day, Sunday; this procession begins on the slopes of the Tor and makes its way to the Abbey. From 1998 these pilgrimages take place on the first Saturday and Sunday of July.

  It has been a bizarre sight on the June weekend in Glastonbury, for that is also the time of the Glastonbury Festival of Contemporary Arts (commonly known as the Glastonbury Festival, and locally as the Pilton Pop Festival, previously the Glastonbury Fayre) when the tiny village of Pilton, five miles from Glastonbury, is invaded by more than 100,000 people from all over the country and abroad. It is now the biggest rock festival in Europe, maybe the world, and Michael

Eavis, farmer and impresario, donates large sums to Greenpeace and other large charities, as well as funding all kinds of local charitable projects. Big-name bands and stars perform; the theatre and circus events can be stunning, green alternative technology and sustainable living structures are on show, and the atmosphere is electric. It is said that if you remember Glastonbury, you weren't there!

In 1996 Michael Eavis began to put on something new for Glastonbury and for a different generation: a Classical Extravaganza in Glastonbury Abbey in mid-August with a reputable national orchestra, choir and military band playing well-known pieces of classical music, the Abbey lit up for the occasion, water displays and fireworks.

There is a Glastonbury Dance Festival at the end of July—a celebration of dance from around the world with dance workshops and dancing in the High Street, all organised locally. And one regular yearly event well worth mentioning is the Glastonbury Children's Festival, organised by Arabella Churchill, who runs the charity Children's World. This festival has been going since 1981, and still remains the only one with a "lost parents tent". However, the variety of fringe and experimental-type puppet, clown and circus shows are well worth a visit by anyone who may still be young-at-heart. It takes place over four days, the last day usually falling on the August bank-holiday Monday.

Something altogether specific to this area, and possibly a relic from an ancient pagan fire festival, is the West Country carnival in mid-November, around Guy Fawkes day. The carnival, with huge illuminated floats made by local clubs to raise money for local charity, tours several Somerset towns and ends up in Glastonbury. A spectacular, crowded, noisy, strangely kitsch procession of illuminated vehicles takes place—enjoyed by everyone.

Scenes from the Glastonbury Festival of
Contemporary Performing Arts, at Pilton

The Anglican pilgrimage in the High Street

GLASTONBURY TOWN

Glastonbury is a small friendly market town with a population of
around 8,000 residents. It has one main High Street, with other shops
scattered along Northload Street, Benedict Street, and Magdalene
Street. It has supermarkets, a Woolworths, a post office, health
centres, churches and chapels, a community school. It used to be
famous for leather and sheepskin goods but it has lost its industrial
backbone now. Clarks, the shoe manufacturer, is headquartered two
miles away in the nearby town of Street, but has cut back
considerably. There is a timber firm, a plastics manufacturer, peat

bogs on the flatlands of the moors (some of it being reclaimed by the Somerset Wildlife Trust), and the lush green pastures of the area used mainly for dairy farming.

History

In the 19th century Glastonbury had a canal linking it with the Parrett estuary which carried cargoes of timber, tiles, slate and coal. Later on the town was part of the Somerset and Dorset Railway—more commonly known as the 'Slow and Dirty'. The town is no longer linked by rail and the nearest station is 12 miles away at Castle Cary.

With its canal and rail link, Glastonbury was a thriving commercial centre in Victorian times, but the 20th century has seen the waning of its industry and the neighbouring town of Street has completely superseded her in terms of material success. Whereas Street enjoys many amenities and Glastonbury has few, most of Glastonbury is a designated Conservation Area with many buildings of great architectural and historical value.

The present

> Every town is special, if only in some respects, but Glastonbury is unique. The town is a major challenge of almost limitless potential: no other small town is known throughout the world, nor for such a variety of reasons; few towns have such a strong religious and spiritual history, none where so much of that heritage remains; no other town lies under a simple hill of such mystical power, and no other town is associated (fairly or unfairly) with one of the world's major music festivals.
>
> —David Williams, Civic Trust Regeneration Unit, 1996

It has been difficult for the local townspeople, who have been here for generations, to live with what they see as a decline in their status. It has been hard for them to accept the large influx of young people with their new ideas about spirituality, and they have feared and resented these newcomers setting up in business and making a living in their town. But gradually, as these 'alternative types' have stayed, brought up their children and sent them to local schools, the ice has thawed and barriers have come down.

In 1996 Mendip District Council invited the Civic Trust to come to Glastonbury and put together a Community Plan for the town as the newly built bypass had created intense unrest. This proved to be a godsend as all the various sections of the community were brought together to thrash out ideas for the future of their town. Somehow, through these meetings and highly charged discussions, the townspeople and the 'alternatives' began to see each other as sharing the same aspirations for Glastonbury. It could be said that a great healing took place.

As a result, all kinds of projects have begun to develop, with an emphasis on improving the environment, creating more facilities for the young and old, restoring areas of the town which were once so beautiful. Of course developers and empire-builders can see the almost limitless potential of Glastonbury and are endlessly proposing vast new complexes and theme parks. But now the townspeople have found their voice, all shades of the community can be involved, and, cross our fingers, good changes are afoot.

Meanwhile, the self-styled magicians, wandering witches, weirdo warlocks, masochistic meditators, and reincarnations of everything from Queen Guinevere to the latest version of Christ, keep coming to 'clean up the energy'. Most of them don't last the course; some stay, though only after going completely mad; it is all a bit of a circus, still feels like living in the middle of a pack of Tarot cards, but life goes on in its mysteriously unpredictable Glastonbury way.

Children's World performers with Arabella Churchill

DIARY OF EVENTS

One could say the seasons are celebrated in Glastonbury just as they were in ancient times, with festivals of all kinds making up the yearly cycle. The following is a list of more or less regular yearly events taking place in Glastonbury.

For more information on dates and venues, contact the Glastonbury Tourist Information Centre, The Tribunal, 9 High Street, Glastonbury, Somerset, BA6 9DP; telephone (01458) 83 2954 or fax 83 2949.

May
Druid gathering
Glastonbury Road Run—6 miles around the Tor

June
Glastonbury Festival of Contemporary Performing Arts—much
    more than pop music, at Worthy Farm, Pilton (last weekend in June)
Flower festival in St John's Church (usually around John-Baptist day)

July
Church of England pilgrimage to the Abbey—solemn Eucharist at
    noon, procession to Evensong at 15.30 (date changes in 1998 to the
    first Saturday in July)
Roman Catholic pilgrimage, from Tor to Abbey (the following Sunday)
Miracles at Glastonbury—medieval-style plays in the Abbey ruins
Glastonbury Dance Festival

August

Glastonbury Arts Festival—wide variety of classical concerts, lectures, exhibitions

Classical Extravaganza—orchestral music in the Abbey

Children's World—four days of fun and entertainment for children (August bank-holiday weekend)

September

Son et Lumière in the Abbey

Tor Fair—traditional travelling fairground

Somerset Arts Week (SAW)—Somerset artists and makers open their studios and workshops to the public with terrific talent on show

November

Glastonbury Carnival—huge illuminated procession (usually the second Saturday in the month)

December

Cutting of the Holy Thorn to send to the Queen for Christmas, by vicar, mayor and schoolchildren in St John's churchyard

There is also a changing programme of events at:
• Somerset Rural Life Museum—exhibitions and demonstrations Telephone (01458) 83 1197
• Peat Moors Visitor Centre—demonstrations and activities (01458) 86 0697
• Isle of Avalon Foundation—talks and courses (01458) 83 3933
• Assembly Rooms Community Arts—music, dance, symposiums (01458) 83 4677
• Chalice Well—quiet and contemplation (01458) 83 1154
• Glastonbury Abbey (01458) 83 4747
• Abbey Retreat House (01458) 83 1112

OPENING TIMES

The information and telephone numbers below are correct at the time of writing. To be sure, contact the Tourist Information Centre.

The Tribunal (Tourist Information Centre)

April–September	Sunday–Thursday	10.00–17.00
	Friday–Saturday	10.00–17.30
October–March	Sunday–Thursday	10.00–16.00
	Friday–Saturday	10.00–16.30

9 High Street, Glastonbury, BA6 8DP; telephone (01458) 83 2954

The Abbey

January	10.00–16.00	July	09.00–17.30
February	10.00–16.30	August	09.00–17.30
March	09.30–17.00	September	09.30–17.30
April	09.30–17.30	October	09.30–16.30
May	09.30–17.30	November	09.30–16.00
June	09.00–17.30	December	10.00–16.00

Those already in the Abbey at closing time will be allowed 30 minutes to leave the premises. Admission prices are posted at the entrance.

Chalice Well

Admission is charged to the well and gardens, which are open daily from April to October 31 from 10.00 to 18.00 and from November to March 31 from midday to 16.00.

The Abbey Barn

For information on events and opening times, as well as admission charges, contact:

> Somerset Rural Life Museum
> Chilkwell Street, Glastonbury, BA6 8DB
> telephone or fax (01458) 83 1197

BIBLIOGRAPHY

Alcock, Leslie
Arthur's Britain, Penguin Press 1971
By South Cadbury is that Camelot?, Thames & Hudson 1972
Ashe, Geoffrey
The Traveller's Guide to Arthurian Britain, Gothic Image
Publications 1997
King Arthur's Avalon, Collins 1957
The Quest for Arthur's Britain (editor and part author), Pall Mall
1968
Camelot and the Vision of Albion, Heinemann 1971
The Virgin, Routledge 1976
Avalonian Quest, Methuen 1982
The Discovery of King Arthur, Doubleday 1985
Mythology of the British Isles, Methuen 1990
King Arthur: the Dream of a Golden Age, Thames & Hudson 1990
Bailey, Alice
The Labours of Hercules, Lucis Trust 1974
Baring-Gould, S
The Holy Grail, Gothic Image 1977
Benham, Patrick
The Avalonians, Gothic Image Publications 1993
Bond, Frederick Bligh
An Architectural Handbook of Glastonbury Abbey, 1909, 1981
The Gate of Remembrance, 1918
The Company of Avalon, 1924
The Glastonbury Scripts, 1925
Bord, Janet and Colin
Mysterious Britain, Garnstone 1972

Briffault, Robert
  The Mothers, Allen & Unwin 1927
Broadhurst, Paul, and Hamish Miller
  The Sun and the Serpent, Pendragon Press 1989
Bromwich, Rachel
  The Welsh Triads, University of Wales Press 1978
Bulleid, Arthur
  The Lake Villages of Somerset, Glastonbury Antiquarian Society 1924
Butler, Alban
  Lives of the Saints, 12 vols, Burns Oates & Washbourne 1926
Caine, Mary
  The Glastonbury Zodiac, Grael Communications 1978
Caldecott, Moyra
  The Green Lady and the King of Shadows: A Glastonbury Legend,
    Gothic Image Publications 1989
Carley, James P
  Glastonbury Abbey: The Holy House at the Head of the Moors Adventurous,
    The Boydell Press 1988, Gothic Image Publications 1996
  John of Glastonbury's 'Cronica' (editor), Boydell 1978
Coles, Bryony and John
  Sweet Track to Glastonbury: the Somerset Levels in Prehistory, Thames
    & Hudson 1986
Cox, Margaret
  The Peat Moors Visitor Centre, Somerset County Council 1993
Critchlow, Keith
  Glastonbury—A Study in Patterns, RILKO 1969
Dames, Michael
  The Silbury Treasure, Thames & Hudson 1976
  The Avebury Cycle, Thames & Hudson 1977
Devereux, Paul
  The New Ley Hunter's Guide, Gothic Image Publications 1994
  Symbolic Landscapes, Gothic Image Publications 1992
Dobson, Rev C.C
  Did Our Lord Visit Britain? Covenant Publishing 1936
Dunning, Robert
  Glastonbury, Alan Sutton 1994
Durdin-Robertson, Lawrence
  The Cult of the Goddess, Cesara Press 1975
  The Goddesses of Chaldaea, Syria and Egypt, Cesara Press 1976

Eliade, Mircea
>*Shamanism: Archaic Techniques of Ecstasy*, Princeton Univ. Press 1964

Evans, Sebastian
>*The High History of the Holy Grail*, Cambridge 1910

Fortune, Dion
>*Avalon of the Heart*, Collins 1938, 1986

Franz, Marie-Louise Von, and Emma Jung
>*The Grail Legend*, 1972

Frazer, James
>*The Golden Bough*, Macmillan 1922

Gasquet, F.A
>*The Last Abbot of Glastonbury*, 1895

Gennaro, Gino
>*The Phenomena of Avalon*, Glastonbury 1979

Geoffrey of Monmouth
>*History of the Kings of Britain*, trans. Lewis Thorpe, Penguin 1966

Gibbs, Ray
>*The Legendary XII Hides of Glastonbury*, Llanerch 1988

Gildas
>*The Ruin of Britain*, trans. Michael Winterbottom in *History from the Sources*, vol 7, Phillimore 1978

Giraldus Cambrensis (Gerald of Wales)
>*The Journey through Wales and The Description of Wales*, trans. Lewis Thorpe, Penguin 1978

Graves, Robert
>*The Greek Myths*, 2 vols, Penguin 1960
>*The White Goddess*, Faber 1952

Graves, Tom
>*Needles of Stone*, Gothic Image Publications 1978
>*Needles of Stone Revisited*, Gothic Image Publications 1986

Harding, Esther
>*Women's Mysteries*, Harper & Row 1976

Hawkes, Jacquetta
>*A Guide to the Prehistoric and Roman Monuments in England and Wales*, Chatto & Windus 1951

Hole, Christina
>*English Folklore*, Batsford 1940

Hoult, Janet
>*A Short History of the Dragon*, Gothic Image Publications, 1978

Hurd, Michael
  Rutland Boughton and the Glastonbury Festivals, Oxford University
      Press 1993
Kindred, Glennie
  The Earth's Cycle of Celebration, Earthkind 1991
Levi-Strauss, Claude
  Introduction to the Science of Mythology, 4 vols, Jonathan Cape 1981
Lewis, Lionel Smithett
  St Joseph of Arimathea at Glastonbury, James Clarke 1922, 1982
London Matriarchy Study Group
  Politics of Matriarchy, 1979
  Menstrual Taboos, 1980
Loomis, Roger Sherman
  The Grail from Celtic Myth to Christian Symbol, University of Wales
      Press 1963
Maltwood, K.E
  A Guide to Glastonbury's Temple of the Stars, 1935, James Clarke 1964
Mann, Nick
  Glastonbury Tor, Glastonbury 1986
Malory, Sir Thomas
  Le Morte d'Arthur, Penguin 1969
  Works, ed. E. Vinaver, 1948
Markale, Jean
  Women of the Celts, Gordon Cremonesi 1975
  King Arthur: King of Kings, Gordon Cremonesi 1977
Matthews, John
  A Glastonbury Reader, Aquarian Press 1991
McCrickard, Janet
  Eclipse of the Sun: An Investigation into Sun and Moon Myths, Gothic
      Image Publications 1990
Michell, John
  New Light on the Ancient Mystery of Glastonbury, Gothic Image
      Publications 1990, 1997
  The Traveller's Guide to Sacred England, Gothic Image Publications
      1996
  The View over Atlantis, 1969, revised as *New View over Atlantis*,
      Thames & Hudson 1983
  City of Revelation, Thames & Hudson 1972
  The Dimensions of Paradise, Thames & Hudson 1988

(with Christine Rhone) *Twelve-Tribe Nations and the Science of Enchanting the Landscape*, Thames & Hudson 1990

Miles, Rosalind
The Women's History of the World, Paladin 1989

Minnitt, Stephen, and John Coles
The Lake Villages of Somerset, Glastonbury Antiquarian Society, Somerset Levels Project and Somerset County Council Museums Service 1996

Moon, Adrian
The First Ground of God, Gothic Image Publications 1978

Nash, D. W
Taliesin, 1858

Neumann, Erich
The Great Mother, Routledge and Kegan Paul 1955, 1970

Pennick, Nigel
The Ancient Science of Geomancy, Thames & Hudson 1979

Perlesvaus (medieval romance) trans. bu Nigel Bryant as *The High Book of the Grail*, Boydell & Brewer 1978

Radford, C. A. Ralegh
The Excavations at Glastonbury Abbey, various dates

Rahtz, Philip
Excavations on Glastonbury Tor, Somerset 1964–66
(and S. Hirst) *Beckery Chapel, Glastonbury, 1967–68* (report on excavation), Glastonbury 1974

Roberts, Anthony
Glastonbury—Ancient Avalon—New Jerusalem, Ryder 1977

Ross, Anne
Everyday Life of the Pagan Celts, Batsford 1970
Pagan Celtic Britain, Sphere Books 1974

Scott, John (ed.)
The Early History of Glastonbury: An Edition, Translation and Study of William of Malmesbury's 'De Antiquitate...' Boydell & Brewer 1981

Shuttle, Penelope, and Redgrove, Peter
The Wise Wound: Menstruation and Everywoman, Gollancz 1978, 1989

Sjoo, Monica
The Religion of the Great Cosmic Mother of All, Harper & Row 1987

Stone, Merlin
The Paradise Papers, Virago 1979
Ancient Mirrors of Womanhood, 2 vols, New Sibylline Books 1979

Thom, A
> *Megalithic Lunar Observatories*, Oxford 1971

Treharne, R. F.
> *The Glastonbury Legends*, Cresset Press 1967

Tudor-Pole, Wellesley
> (and Rosalind Lehmann) *A Man Seen Afar*, Neville Spearman 1965
> (ed.) *Michael, Prince of Heaven*, 1951

Wade-Evans, A. W
> *Nennius' History of the Britons*, SPCK 1938

Warner, Marina
> *Alone of All Her Sex: The Myth and Cult of the Virgin Mary*, Quartet
>   1978

Watkin, Aelred
> "Glastonbury 1538–9", in *Downside Review* 1949

Watkins, Alfred
> *The Old Straight Track*, Methuen 1974

Weston, Jessie
> *From Ritual to Romance*, Cambridge University Press 1920

Westwood, Jennifer
> *Albion: A Guide to Legendary Britain*, Granada 1985

William of Malmesbury, see Scott, J.

The books listed here, unless they are out of print, are available at
Gothic Image bookshop, 7 High Street, Glastonbury, Somerset,
BA6 9DP—telephone (+44 1458) 83 1453, fax 83 1666—or by
mail order from the same address. We can send books anywhere in the
world.

INDEX

GOTHIC IMAGE
PUBLICATIONS

The Avalonians
Patrick Benham

The New Ley Hunter's Guide
Paul Devereux

Conflict in the Caucasus
Svetlana Chervonnaya

New Light on the Ancient Mystery of Glastonbury
John Michell

Devas, Fairies and Angels
William Bloom

Dowsing the Crop Circles
edited by John Michell

Positively Wyrd: Harnessing the Chaos in your Life
Tom Graves

Dragons: Their History and Symbolism
Janet Hoult

Robin Hood: Green Lord of the Wildwood
John Matthews

Fogou
Jo May

The Sacred Magician: A Ceremonial Diary
William Bloom

Glastonbury Abbey
James Carley

The Glastonbury Tor Maze
Geoffrey Ashe

Saint or Satan? Russia's New Rasputin, Anatoly Kashpirovsky
Galina Vinogradova

The Green Lady and the King of Shadows
Moyra Caldecott

Spiritual Dowsing
Sig Lonegren

Labyrinths: Ancient Myths and Modern Uses
Sig Lonegren

Symbolic Landscapes: The Dreamtime Earth and Avebury's Open Secret
Paul Devereux

The Living World of Faery
R J Stewart

Traveller's Guide to Arthurian Britain
Geoffrey Ashe

Meditation in a Changing World
William Bloom

Traveller's Guide to Sacred England
John Michell

Needles of Stone Revisited
Tom Graves

Wyrd Allies
Tom Graves

Gothic Image Publications are available from all good bookshops
or direct from
GOTHIC IMAGE PUBLICATIONS
7 High Street • Glastonbury, Somerset • England • BA6 9DP
Telephone +44 1458 83 1453 • (Fax +44 1458 83 1666)

GOTHIC IMAGE TOURS

Gothic Image organises tours around the sacred sites of Glastonbury, including the Tor, the Abbey, Wearyall Hill, Chalice Well and Gog and Magog.

Tours are 2½ hours in duration; parties are small and friendly and are accompanied by an expert on the history, myths, legends and spritual tradition of each place.

One-day trips are organised to nearby sites such as Cadbury Camelot, Avebury, Silbury, Stonehenge (with special access), Tintagel and Stanton Drew stone circle. Longer journeys, of 10 and 14 days, visit the further reaches of Scotland and Ireland including Iona, the Orkney Islands, Newgrange, the Skelligs and the Aran Islands. Along the way we explore and discover our ancient spiritual heritage.

All tours are by arrangement and can be designed to suit your particular group. For further information contact Jamie George at the bookshop:

> Gothic Image
> 7 High Street
> Glastonbury, Somerset, England
> BA6 9DP
> *telephone* (01458) 831453, *fax* 831666
> *email* idea@isleofavalon.co.uk